MAR

NOR MANDY

with Local Tips
*The author's special recommendations are
highlighted in yellow throughout this guide*

There are six symbols to help you find your way around this guide:

Marco Polo's top recommendations

sites with a great view

where the local people meet

where young people get together

(A1)
map references

follow this route on the map for the best sights in Normandy

MARCO ⊕ POLO

Other travel guides and language guides in this series:

Algarve • Amsterdam • Australia • Brittany • California
Costa Brava/Barcelona • Costa del Sol/Granada • Côte d'Azur • Crete
Cuba • Cyprus • Florence • Florida • Gran Canaria • Greek Islands
Ireland • Istanbul • Mallorca • Malta • New York • New Zealand
Paris • Prague • Rhodes • Rome • South Africa • Tenerife
Turkish Coast • Tuscany • Venice

French • German • Italian • Spanish

*Marco Polo would be very interested to hear your
comments and suggestions. Please write to:*

*World Leisure Marketing Ltd
Marco Polo Guides
9 Downing Road, West Meadows
Derby DE21 6HA England*

*Cover photograph: Mont-Saint-Michel (Schapowalow/Huber)
Photographs: Amberg (93), The Art and History Archive, Berlin (16), Bauer (43);
Frei (7, 11, 23, 29, 35, 40, 56, 58, 67, 68, 71, 72); Friedrichsmeier (8, 18, 24, 26);
Kallabis (inside front cover, 4); Lange (20);
Reiser (14, 30, 44, 48, 50, 61, 64, 75, 82, 86, 90); Schuster (37); Thomas (49, 52)*

*1st English edition 1998
© Mairs Geographischer Verlag, Ostfildern Germany
Author: Hans-Peter Reiser
Translation: Alison Layland
Editorial director: Ferdinand Ranft
Design and layout: Thienhaus/Wipperman
Printed in Italy*

CONTENTS

Discover Normandy

A lively coast and tranquil inland region

The essence of Normandy's charm lies in the variety of its landscape and the fact that the way of life here is still so firmly rooted in agricultural tradition. Those who are familiar with the journey from Calais or Boulogne to Paris, can be forgiven for thinking that Normandy is rather flat and dull. Once you veer off this route, however, it soon becomes clear that the scenery you have glimpsed from the train or car window is by no means characteristic of an otherwise varied and captivating countryside.

The coastal landscape is a combination of rugged cliffs lashed by breakers and flat sandy beaches washed over by gentle lapping waves. It is punctuated all the way along with busy ports, historic villages and old-fashioned seaside towns. The hinterland is a patchwork of hedgerows, lush meadows grazed by placid cows, hills and valleys, forests and rivers, and endless fields and apple orchards.

The spectacular cliff formations of Étretat: the Porte and the Aiguille d'Aval

It is a region steeped in history and rich in architectural treasures, not to mention its enviable gastronomic heritage.

Normandy is sandwiched between Picardy to the east and Brittany to the west and is divided into five *départements* (similar to English counties). These are Seine-Maritime and Eure (Haute-Normandie) which cover an area of 12 258 sq km, and Calvados, Manche and Orne (Basse-Normandie) covering 17 583 sq km. The total population of the region is around 3.2 million and its capital is Rouen.

The eastern stretch of the Normandy coast begins around the little fishing port of Le Tréport which lies on the borders of Normandy and Picardy. The section between Dieppe and Étretat is known as the Côte d'Albâtre (Alabaster Coast), where the edge of the Pays de Caux chalk plateau plunges into the sea. This shoreline is gradually receding as the sea is eroding the tall white cliffs at a rapid rate. Over time the tireless pounding of the waves has sculpted the soft rocks into some weird and wonderful shapes. The most striking of these cliffs can be seen around Étretat: the Falaise d'Amont to the east of the resort, and the Falaise d'Aval to the west are prominent coastal landmarks. The most dramatic rock formation of all along here is the Aiguille – a huge 700-m 'needle' that shoots out of the sea.

Over the millennia, the rivers of this corner of northern France have carved their way through the plateau, forming gentle valleys. Major ports such as Dieppe, fishing villages and numerous seaside resorts like Fécamp and Veulettes-sur-Mer, developed on the fertile land around the mouths of these rivers.

The Côte d'Alabâtre hinterland is known as the Pays de Caux. Along with the Pays de Bray to the east, this inland area is perfectly adapted to cultivating crops and rearing livestock, and there are signs of agricultural activity at every turn. Near Longueville, the air is redolent with the distinctive and pleasant aroma from the cider-bottling plants, and the equally distinctive smells emanating from the cheese-making factories waft through the air near Neufchâtel-en-Bray.

The western edge of the chalk plateau is bounded by the wide Val de Seine. Both economically and historically, the River Seine is one of Normandy's most significant natural features. It was, and still is, one of the most important trade routes of northern France. Many of its loops encircle commercial and industrial centres, and extensive sections of its banks are lined with industrial buildings.

The Seine's commercial importance, however, does not overshadow the beauty and interest of its valley. The river flows from Paris into Normandy via the Eure département. Winding its way slowly to the sea, it goes past impressive chalk cliffs, through the historic city of Rouen, past quiet monasteries and abbeys and through the woods of the Forêt de Brotonne. After its meanderings, the river finally reaches the sea in the broad Baie de la Seine, near Le Havre where it forms the boundary of the Seine-Maritime département.

The river is at its most enchanting along the southern reaches where it passes through the Eure region. This stretch runs from the village of Giverny, where Monet created his famous gardens, to the rocks of Les Andelys, where Richard the Lionheart built his great fortress, the Château Gaillard, in defiance of the French king Philippe-Auguste.

The Pays d'Ouche is an area which extends to the west of the Seine and at its heart lies the peaceful town of Evreux. Centred around the historic Notre Dame cathedral, this prosperous market town has developed into the focal point of the surrounding area, yet it has managed to conserve its quiet rural character. Extensive meadowlands, fields and the thick woodland of the Parc Naturel Régional de Brotonne, blanket the countryside between here and the Côte de Grâce, a cheerful piece of coast by the Seine estuary that bustles with tourist activity in summer.

The historic port of Honfleur lies across the Baie de la Seine from Le Havre and marks the beginning of the département of Calvados. The Corniche Normande is the picturesque stretch of coast which runs for about 20 km from Honfleur to Trouville where the Côte Fleurie (Coast of Flowers) begins. Every year, the chic resort of Deauville draws flocks of well-heeled holidaymakers to its shores. Its social calendar is full during the high season, especially in August when most of the activity is focused on equestrian events. International jet-setters and wealthy Parisians congregate at the casino and racecourse, lounge around in luxury hotels and parade along the promenade (Les Planches) in their latest designer wear.

Although it was a fashionable resort when its neighbour across the river was just a fishing village,

Trouville is now considered something of a poor relation to Deauville, even though it has its own wide beach, ornate seaside villas, pavement brasseries, boardwalk and casino.

Continuing west along the coast, past Cabourg which marks the end of the Côte Fleurie, the resorts become less crowded and more informal than their upmarket counterparts. This last section of coast before the Cotentin peninsula is called the Côte de Nacre, but is more commonly known as the *Plages du Débarquement* or the D-Day Beaches. It is an area of great historic importance as it was here, on June 6 1944, that the Allied forces

Cabourg: Marcel Proust's summer retreat

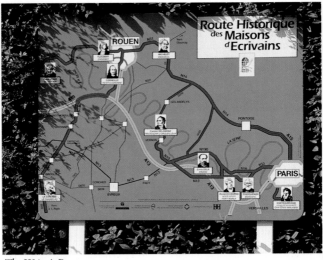

The Writer's Route

landed and began the liberation of France and Europe. The landing sites of Omaha Beach and Utah Beach, with their shell-pitted cliff-tops and vast cemeteries, evoke vivid images of the war. It is impossible to forget the bloody Battle of Normandy, which was not just fought on the beaches but all through the region. As the troops advanced, fierce conflicts ensued over every metre of Norman soil. There was hardly a town or village which did not experience its hour of grief, suffering terrible human losses and destruction. It took two months before Rouen was freed, thus liberating Normandy and heralding the end of World War II. All along the coast and in the inland towns memorials and museums keep alive the memory of those fateful events.

The département of Calvados is the agricultural heart of Normandy, centred around the fertile Pays d'Auge. The lush pastureland is scattered with dappled cows, the black and white Norman breed prized for its meat and creamy milk. Apple trees grow everywhere, both wild and in vast cultivated orchards. Cheeses, butter, cider and Calvados apple brandy are the mainstays of the local economy.

The three cities of Calvados — Bayeux, Caen and Lisieux — are all of historic and architectural importance. Bayeux is a name ingrained in many minds from early school days alongside the date of 1066 and the Norman Conquest. This medieval town was one of the few places lucky enough to escape destruction during World War II. Its historic streets, cathedral and ancient tapestry draw tourists and school parties all year round. Caen was the capital of the duchy of Normandy under William the Conqueror. Unlike Bayeux, the city was devastated in the war, but many of its historic buildings were restored. The city of Lisieux, with its Norman Gothic cathedral, was the home of Sainte Thérèse and is a very important place of pilgrimage.

The most westerly département of Normandy is the Manche. Rectangular in shape and with a very diverse landscape, this area lends itself perfectly to a circular tour. The scenic route rounds the Cotentin peninsula, heading north up the eastern side to the Pointe de Barfleur, across the northern coast past the deep-water port of Cherbourg to the other 'corner' at the Cap de la Hague, and down past the towering cliffs of Nez de la Jobourg all the way along the western side to the spectacular Baie du Mont-Saint-Michel on the Normandy/Brittany boundary. This huge rock, crowned by the 8th-century abbey, is one of the region's most spectacular sites. With its wave-lashed cliffs, deserted beaches and a succession of historic buildings, the landscape along this route begins to take on the characteristics of the wilder, rockier Breton coast. The inland region is no less interesting, but remains relatively undiscovered. In winter it is windswept and bleak, yet in late spring and summer the heathland is transformed by a profusion of colourful flowers.

Those who are drawn to the sea and sand at holiday time will not be disappointed by the fine beaches of the Normandy coast. Nature-lovers, on the other hand, will derive the most pleasure touring the inland areas, especially the Orne. The unspoilt beauty of this peaceful département is still relatively unknown,

mainly because tourists tend to pass through it en route to the coast or the better-known neighbouring regions. Orne shares its Suisse Normande beauty spot in the north with Calvados, and the Parc Naturel Régional Normandie-Maine in the south with the neighbouring region of Maine. In between lies La Perche, an equally picturesque area which bridges the two different landscapes, giving the département its unique character. Shaped by hills and valleys, woods and meadows, hedges and bushes, the countryside here is perfect for walking, riding and cycling tours.

But Normandy is more than just a picturesque combination of lively coast, agricultural plains and a peaceful rural hinterland. It has a life, character and history of its own built up over centuries. The region was part of ancient Gaul and inhabited by Celts until it was conquered by Julius Caesar in the 1st century BC and incorporated into the Roman Empire. As Roman authority waned, the Franks led by King Clovis took over power towards the end of the 5th century. Then in the 8th century the Viking raids on the coast began. Initially the Norsemen came on sporadic raids, looting the settlements and returning home with their booty. Gradually, however, they began to settle and in 911 a treaty was signed between the Norse leader Rollo and the Frankish king Charles III. Rollo was made first Duke of Normandy and the power of the duchy quickly increased. In 1066, Duke William conquered England and was crowned there as William I. After his death, the disputes among his sons over succession divided Normandy and England. The territorial fight continued for centuries. In 1415 Henry V won a decisive victory at the Battle of Agincourt and the English held Normandy until 1450. It wasn't until after Joan of Arc's victory at Orléans, which signalled the end of the Hundred Years' War (1337-1453), that the last of the English were finally expelled and Normandy was firmly integrated into the rest of France. The next historic event of major importance on Norman soil occurred centuries later with the Allied landings in 1944, which marked the beginning of the end of World War II.

This fascinating history is reflected in the art, culture and, above all, the architecture of the region. Normandy boasts an incredible architectural heritage and a number of excellent historical routes have been put together for visitors who want a deeper understanding of the region and its past. You can either base your holiday itinerary around these well-planned tours or use them as an alternative, more interesting way of getting from A to B. Maps and descriptions are provided by the local tourist offices. One of the best examples is the *Route du Val de Seine et des Abbayes*, which concentrates on the Seine valley and its abbeys. It leads from Rouen to Le Havre, through an ever-changing scenery of chalk cliffs, hills and forests. The route begins in the regional capital with the Abbaye Saint-Ouen, leading to Saint-Martin-de-Boscherville and the Abbaye Saint-Georges, then on to the ruins of the Abbaye Jumièges and the Abbaye Saint-Wandrille, finally coming to the Abbaye Valasse in Gruchet-le-Valasse and finishing with the Abbaye Saint-Sauveur in Montivilliers. This route covers just a few of the many splendid abbeys in the region. Characterized by their towers and turrets, most of them were founded in the 11th century. Other typical examples include the Abbaye aux Hommes in Caen, the Abbaye Saint-Trinité in Lessay, the Abbaye Notre-Dame-de-Bernay, the oldest ecclesiastical building in Normandy, and the Cistercian Abbaye de Mortemer. The undisputed highlight among all these magnificent buildings, however, is the Mont-Saint-Michel. Standing on top of a huge granite rock that rises out of the sea, this legendary abbey is one of the most prized architectural treasures in the country.

In addition to its numerous abbeys and monasteries, Normandy has more than its fair share of cathedrals, which collectively illustrate the various architectural styles and developments of the Middle Ages. The pointed arches that typify the Early Gothic style, for example, can be seen in the small cathedral of St Pierre in Lisieux; the twin-towered façade, high nave and lantern tower so characteristic of the Gothic style are exemplified in Evreux, Rouen, Coutances, Fécamp and Bayeux; and the Flamboyant style which developed from the late Gothic and early Renaissance, is reflected in the church of Verneuil-sur-Arve.

Another popular historical tour is the *Route Normandie-Vexin* which takes in some of the finest Norman castles, but also passes the Cistercian monastery of Fontaine-Guérard, the Abbey of

The Notre-Dame cathedral in Rouen: a Gothic masterpiece

Mortemer and the church of Vernon, the Archaeological Museum of Guiry-en-Vexin and the gardens of Giverny. The cities of Rouen and Lyons-la-Forêt have also been included in this route because of their many historic sights. The main highlights, however, are the châteaux of Martainville, Vascoeuil, Gisors, Boury, Ambleville, Gaillard-les-Andelys and Bizy.

The sheer number of castles and fortified manors found in Normandy are a testament to the endless military conflicts which the Normans were engaged in during the Middle Ages. The earlier strongholds were centred around a keep, the *donjon*, which was initially square-shaped and later became round. The Norman *manoirs* evolved in more peaceful times, when the design of buildings was no longer just functional. Though the complexes were still fortified, appearance became as important as practicality, hence the introduction of half-timbering, decorative brickwork, colour and pattern. These early feudal seats were the forerunners of the grand châteaux which followed. Their design was largely influenced by the ornate Italian Renaissance style illustrated to perfection in the Château d'O and Fontaine-Henry. The splendid palaces in Evreux (Palais Épiscopal) and Rouen (Palais de Justice), also built in this period, were designed to show off the power and wealth of the nobility.

The second wave of construction which followed the Wars of Religion was predominantly Baroque, leaning more towards austerity and symmetry. Gardens were an integral feature of these great mansions and were laid out in the geometric French style. The Château Balleroy and the Château Cany are two of the finest examples.

Next came Classicism with its simple, uncluttered lines. The gardens and parks which surrounded these Châteaux were instead laid out in the English fashion. The best exponent of this style is Château Sassy with its beautifully kept gardens designed to appear as if nature has been left to its own devices.

The *Route Historique des Maisons d'Écrivains* follows the trail of famous writers who lived here, through the countryside which inspired their writing. The houses, holiday homes and favourite haunts of François Châteaubriand, Alexandre Dumas, Gustave Flaubert, Victor Hugo, Guy de Maupassant, Marcel Proust, Emile Zola and many others can be visited along the way.

Their literary predecessors were the studious monks in the medieval abbeys, who busied themselves producing beautiful manuscripts in Latin glorifying the deeds of the Norman dukes. They were followed by chroniclers such as Ordericus Vitalis and Robert of Torigni. Over the centuries Norman writers continued the tradition of documenting ideas and systems of thought. Alexis de Tocqueville, following a trip to America, pondered long and hard on the fortunes and the future of democratic societies in his book *On Democracy in America*.

Normandy also inspired many painters, although they have so far not been commemorated in a specially dedicated route. The first to fall under the spell of the soft light and unique imagery of the region was the 17th-century artist Nicolas Poussin. The movement that really epitomizes Normandy, however, is Impressionism. Gustave Courbet was inspired by the white cliffs of Étretat and Eugène Boudin by the pretty harbour at Honfleur. Boudin merits a special place in the history of the movement. Born in Honfleur, the son of a ship's captain, he preferred to paint his seascapes and coastal scenes in the open air rather than in a studio. He was inspired by the movement of the waves, the changing skies and the effects of light on the landscape. In his own words '…three brushstrokes from nature are worth more than two days studio work at an easel.'

Numerous painters followed his example, thus giving rise to the 'School of Honfleur' which included Jean-Frédéric Bazille, Alfred Sisley and, most significantly, Claude Monet, some of whose best works – namely the Rouen Cathedral and water lily series – were painted in Normandy. Monet spent his childhood in Le Havre and the last years of his life in his garden retreat at Giverny which has been carefully restored and is now open to visitors.

Painters who followed subsequent movements were similarly influenced by the qualities of light and landscape. Among them were Georges Seurat, Raoul Dufy and Georges Braque, who is buried in the cemetery at Varengeville. Examples of the work of all these great artists can be seen in Normandy's many art museums.

One final tour worth singling out is the *Stud Farm and Châteaux Route*. This passes through the Orne département and takes in a succession of elegant châteaux and stud farms, including the world-famous Haras National du Pin.

There are many other tours worth investigating: the *Ivory and Spice Route*, the *Route of the Dukes*, the *Glassblowers' Route*, the *Cheese and Cider Route*… few places can claim to cater for so many interests as Normandy does.

History at a glance

3000 BC
First settlers come to the region

1000 BC
Celts settle in Normandy

56 BC
Julius Caesar conquers Gaul. Caen, Coutances, Lisieux and Rouen are among the earliest Roman towns to be founded

2nd century AD
The beginning of the spread of Christianity. Rouen becomes the first bishopric

486
The Merovingian King Clovis conquers the Romans at Soissons

6th/7th century
Numerous churches and monasteries are founded, including Mont-Saint-Michel in 709

8th century
Viking raids on Normandy. Town and countryside are plundered and devastated

911
The treaty of St-Clair-sur-Épte grants settlement rights to the Vikings, and their leader, Rollo, is made first Duke of Normandy

1066
Following his victory at Hastings, William the Conqueror claims the English throne. The combined Anglo-Norman power poses a threat to the Frankish kings

1196
Richard the Lionheart builds the Château Gaillard as a defence against the French

1204
The Anglo-Norman kingdom breaks up and the Duchy of Normandy reverts to a French province

1337-1453
The Hundred Years' War between France and England

1431
Joan of Arc is burnt at the stake in Rouen

1486
Normandy is finally and permanently annexed to France

1639
Increased taxes lead to a revolt which is put down by Cardinal Richelieu

1806
The continental trade barriers imposed by Napoleon against England badly affect Norman maritime trade

1920
Joan of Arc is canonized by the Vatican

1940-44
Normandy is occupied by German troops. 1942 sees the first attempt at liberation by the Allies at Dieppe

1944
The Allied Invasions on the Normandy beaches. Numerous towns and cities are destroyed, but France is finally liberated

1974
Mont-Saint-Michel becomes a national monument

Bayeux to D-Day

Jeanne d'Arc to Monet; Gothic and lace

The Bayeux Tapestry

The amazingly well preserved Bayeux tapestry is a work of great historic value. It provides us with a detailed visual account of the first spectacular cross-Channel invasion that took place, 900 years before the Allied invasions. It starts with King Harold's visit to Normandy and ends with the Battle of Hastings and the conquest of England by Duke William of Normandy in 1066. The whole story is told from a Norman point of view and portrays the Saxons and their king as the evildoers. The tapestry is, in fact, a huge linen strip (70 m long and 50 cm wide) embroidered with 58 images which give an impression as vivid as any photograph of both the events themselves and of day-to-day life in Norman times. Originally hung in the cathedral nave, the Bayeux tapestry is now exhibited in the Centre Guillaume le Conquérant, an 18th-century Jesuit seminary

With its elegant half-timbered houses Étretat is one of Normandy's most charming coastal resorts

converted specifically for the purpose of coping with the constant stream of visitors. There are rooms with excellent films and displays providing the background and history to the events. When it comes to viewing the tapestry itself, visitors can listen to a commentary on individual headsets which explains in detail the images of this fascinating medieval comic strip.

Camembert

The tradition of cheese-making in the Pays d'Auge goes back hundreds of years. The area is now renowned all over the world for its cheeses, the most famous of which is Camembert. Because it was never patented, the 'Camembert' name can be used by anyone and, due to its huge popularity, Camembert imitations flood the world market. Genuine Camembert is marked with the VCN (*Véritable Camembert Normand*) stamp of authenticity and comes from the centre of the region's cheese-making activities, Vimoutiers, just 4 km from the village of Camembert, where the illustrious cheese was 'invented'. Legend has it that a priest, fleeing from his persecutors during the French Revolution, gave his treasured cheese-making recipe to Madame Marie Harel who had sheltered him, as a token of his gratitude. She passed the recipe down to her daughter, who took the business very seriously, and began to market the cheese packed in straw. Her endeavours were aided by the support of no less a patron than Napoleon III, who had developed a taste for this new soft cheese which he discovered while on a trip to Argentan, thus spreading its renown to court circles. The success of the product was hindered by the inability to keep it fresh, but a solution was finally found in the form of the chipboard box invented by Auguste Lepetit. Currently, 30 million Camemberts per year are sold all over the world.

D-Day

Following Operation Jubilee in August 1942, an abortive attempt to land a 5000-strong commando unit in Dieppe, the Allies had to accept that it would take more than a single raid to break through the tight German defence lines. During this attempt to capture the port and establish a bridgehead in France, 3350 soldiers were captured or killed.

Two years later, Operation Overlord was planned down to the last minute detail and everything meticulously prepared. The Allies had decided to concentrate their combined strength on breaking through the Atlantic defences on the flat beaches of the Côte de Nacre and the Cotentin peninsula. From west to east the beach divisions were code-named Utah, Omaha, Gold, Juno and Sword. On June 6 1944, one day later than planned because of bad weather, the storming of the Plages du Débarquement, the D-Day Beaches, went underway. Over 136 000 troops were transported across the Channel in 7000 boats. There followed a series of bitter conflicts which came to a head in the dreadful battle at

D-Day, 6 June 1944: the Allied forces land in Normandy

Falaise, where the Germans took their last stand in August 1944. The occupation of Normandy was not ended, however, until the recapture of Rouen on 30 August 1944. The price of final victory was high: almost 100 000 lives had been lost among them 37 000 Allied soldiers, and most of the towns and villages, were almost completely destroyed.

The vast war cemeteries with their endless rows of white crosses and the forlorn remains of pill-boxes and memorials along the coast are moving reminders of Normandy's 'longest day'.

Flamboyant

The style of architecture most associated with Normandy is the Flamboyant variant of the Late Gothic. Around the end of the 15th century, while most architects in Europe were turning to the Renaissance, craftsmen in Normandy continued to adhere to the Flamboyant style until well after the end of the Hundred Years' War. The playful filigree ornamentation which character-izes this style can be seen at its most impressive in the Tour du Beurre of Rouen cathedral and the decoration of the cathedral at Evreux.

Half-timbered houses

The half-timbered farmhouses of Normandy are the embodiment of history and native tradition, and can be found in practically every Norman town or village. The local style is characterized by long, parallel vertical timbers, with lovely infill designs in her-ringbone or St Andrew's cross patterns. These black and white rustic buildings contrast beauti-fully with the profusion of flowers that surrounds them and are usu-ally set against a background of meadows, grazing cows and apple orchards. They make very photo-genic subjects and you'll find it hard to resist snapping away.

Joan of Arc

Jeanne d'Arc, known as the 'Maid of Orléans' or 'La Pucelle', is one of the most legendary figures in French history and is still consid-ered the patron saint of France. This extraordinary young country girl was born during the Hundred Years' War (1337-1453), a long and protracted struggle between France and England for the French throne, which plunged the land into terror and despair. Much of the fighting took place on Norman soil, and the young Joan must have experienced its horrors and deprivation. In 1415, the English King Henry V and his army defeated the French at the Battle of Agincourt and won back the Duchy of Normandy. The French army was demoralized and the outcome of the war seemed to have been decided. The reversal of fortunes, how-ever, which led to the ultimate French victory, was brought about by Joan of Arc.

Born in 1412 in Domrémy la Pucelle in Lorraine, the daughter of a farmer, Joan felt from a very young age that she had a divine calling to free her country from war. She declared that St Michael, St Catherine and St Margaret had all told her to expel the English from French soil. She succeeded on her second attempt in con-vincing the Dauphin – the French hereditary heir – of her mission. In 1429, aged just 17, she

Statue of Joan of Arc, the French national heroine, in Pennedepie

led a 3000-strong army into battle and freed Orléans from the surrounding English forces. On 16 July of that year Charles VII was crowned King of France in Reims. Other victories ensued, but she failed to recapture Paris and in May 1430 she was taken prisoner by the Burgundians, who were fighting on the side of the enemy. The English set up a tribunal of bishops and abbots in Rouen, presided over by Pierre Cauchon, later the Bishop of Lisieux, and she was found guilty of witchcraft and heresy. On 30 May 1431 she was burnt at the stake on the Place du Vieux-Marché. She received no assistance from Charles VII, whom she had helped win the throne. It was not until 20 years later, when

he took Rouen, that he reversed the judgement.

It was Joan of Arc's patriotism which helped inspire the French troops to ultimately win the long war. She was canonized by the Vatican in 1920.

Claude Monet

It was the soft, changing quality of the light which attracted many painters to the coast of Normandy in the middle of the 19th century. Honfleur and Étretat both became artists' colonies. Eugène Boudin formed the School of Honfleur in the town of his birth and founded the Impressionist movement which was to have a profound influence on European painting. It was Boudin who gave Monet guidance in the early stages of his painting career. Claude Monet became one of the foremost exponents of Impressionism, and the movement was fittingly named after one of his early paintings, *Impression: Sunrise*. Born in Paris in 1840, he grew up in Le Havre where Boudin encouraged him to paint out of doors. He spent the latter part of his life in Giverny where he created a beautiful garden which became the subject-matter of many of his paintings. He died here in 1926 at the age of 86, and is buried in Giverny cemetery.

Needlepoint lace

The skilful twining of threads around needles affixed to a lace-making cushion is a technique which originated in Flanders. Brussels lace was soon overtaken by Venetian needlepoint designs which were extremely expensive and naturally highly favoured by French court society. In order to stop the flow of money towards Venice, imports were banned and a lacemaking centre was established by royal decree in Alençon. It soon developed its own unique form, characterized by heavily contoured ornamentation on a delicate, hand-sewn, open-weave background. The enduring popularity of Norman lace is due to the beautiful Point d'Alençon design created by Madame la Perrière. In the 19th century, machine-made lace gradually replaced the more costly and labour-intensive handcrafted version. The art of lacemaking is well documented in the Museums of Alençon and Argentan, the main centres of a once thriving industry.

Normans

Settled by the Celts, then colonized by the Romans, Normandy's first real ancestors were the Vikings. Travelling in their longboats from Scandinavia, they raided the land time and again. It was not just Normandy which bore the brunt of their attacks; whole tracts of Europe trembled before them. It certainly appears, however, that they had a distinct preference for this region, whose coast and wide rivers seemed to have been made for their waterborne tactics. They would appear suddenly in their small, manoeuvrable ships, spreading fear before them, plunder anything they could lay their hands on, and disappear as swiftly as they had come. Nowhere was safe, be it monasteries, abbeys, villages or towns. Over the course of time, however, the Vikings began to weary of the raids, and all the comings and goings which they entailed. They started to settle

and colonize the lands they had hitherto been plundering. This meant they were more open to counter-attack by the local people, and consequently they had to work out new systems of defence. At the beginning of the 10th century they formed a powerful force under the leadership of their commander, Rollo. The Frankish king, Charles le Simple was wise enough to accept the new balance of power, and in 911 he concluded the treaty of St-Clair-sur-Épte with the Norse leader, which granted the invaders settlement rights over a broad area around the Seine. Rollo was eventually baptized a Christian, changed his name to Robert and became the first Duke of Normandy. The Norsemen soon after began to breed cattle and establish communities, fending off attacks from other marauding Vikings. This was really the birth of the province, which was followed by a period of relative peace and stability, and rapid development.

Trou normand

Calvados is held in the same high regard in Normandy as whisky is in Scotland. This strong brandy distilled from apples is drunk as a *digestif*, the perfect end to any Norman meal. In many restaurants, a generous glass of Calvados is often served in between courses. Known as the *trou normand* — the 'Norman hole' — it is meant to clear your palate and help you digest in preparation for the next dish. If you decide to indulge in this tradition, you may well find yourself at the end of a three-course meal with a lighter head and emptier pocket than you intended.

Dining à la normande

*Cream, butter and apples are prominent features
of a rich and hearty cuisine*

When French cuisine was seeking to reinvent itself, the regional cuisine of Normandy remained resolutely unchanged. The nouvelle cuisine trends that swept the country made little impact on the eating habits of the obstinate Normans who are justifiably proud of their long culinary tradition. And a good job too, for it would be a sad thing to lose the many and varied combinations of full-flavoured ingredients which typify the robust and hearty *cuisine normande*.

It has to be said, however, that it is not the healthiest of cooking styles. The typical *sauce normande*, while delicious, is crammed with calories and cholesterol. Butter, cream, Calvados and above all crème fraîche are the mainstays of the rich dishes, as is the irresistible rich flavour of Camembert. So, unless you have a will of iron, it's not the easiest of places to watch your waistline.

The busy fishing ports that line the Normandy coast supply fresh fish and shellfish to all the markets of France. Not surprisingly, fish is a central feature on most restaurant menus. The *fruits de mer* platter is a rich mixture of oysters, lobster, prawns, mussels, crab, scallops and any other available shellfish – some raw, some cooked – all colourfully arranged on a large plate. Other local seafood specialities include oysters (*huîtres*) served with a shallot and wine vinegar sauce; *demoiselles de Cherbourg*, baby lobsters cooked in their own stock flavoured with Calvados and served with butter; or *marmite dieppoise*, a delicious fish casserole made with several varieties of fish, such as turbot and sole, shellfish, vegetables, cider, butter and a generous helping of cream. Mussels are always popular and are prepared in a variety of ways typical of the region: *moules marinières* are mussels steamed with shallots, parsley and butter; *moules bernevalaise* are cooked in a cider and shallot sauce.

The inland rivers are teeming with all the varieties of freshwater fish any seasoned gourmet could wish for. Trout is either steamed

*'Fruits de mer' take pride of place
on the Norman menu*

21

and served with a fine sauce, usually flavoured with Calvados, or else prepared *à la dieppoise*, with shrimps, mussels, mushrooms and cider or white wine. Sole, another favourite, is often cooked with mussels, shrimps, onions, vegetables, eggs, cream and herbs.

The Normans are equally fond of meat, especially the more gamey varieties. Dishes based on pork, rabbit, lamb and duck feature on most menus. The queen of meat dishes is *canard à la rouennaise*, roast duck with a sauce made of the blood, red wine and a dash of Calvados. *Pré-salé* lamb is widely acclaimed. The sheep feed off the aromatic herbs which grow on the salt marshes around the Baie du Mont Saint Michel giving the meat its unique delicate flavour. A typical speciality is roast leg of lamb (*gigot d'agneau*) served with a cider and cream sauce.

The most commonly used cooking fat aside from butter is *graisse normande* — rendered pork and beef fat simmered with vegetables and herbs. It is the key ingredient in a good *soupe normande*, which is made of haricot beans, leeks, cabbage and potatoes.

The region is also known for its variety of *charcuterie*. Foremost among the many types of sausage is the *boudin noir* from Mortagne-au-Perche, an exceptional black pudding which is well seasoned and often served with fried onions on a bed of apple rings. Its counterpart, the *boudin blanc*, is made from poultry, veal or fish with eggs, milk and cream. Other local specialities include the delicious, spicy *andouillette* and the smoked *andouilles*, a speciality of Vire, both of which are made with tripe. Pâtés, terrines and *rillettes* (potted pork) are also integral to the Norman diet.

Normandy produces over 30 varieties of cheese and is not surprisingly known as *la région des fromages*. Calvados is the main cheese-making region and production is centred around the Pays d'Auge. Camembert accounts for 90% of the region's cheese production. Although imitation camemberts are sold all around the world, only the genuine cheeses, made with the milk of Normandy cows, are given the VCN (*Véritable Camembert Normand*) stamp. Among the other excellent cheeses are Livarot, a well-seasoned cheese with a red rind, which 'runs' when it is cut and the Neufchâtel from the Pays de Bray, which is mild and creamy beneath its white crust. The leader of the pack, also in terms of price, is the square-shaped Pont l'Evêque, whose yellowish rind

---

A matter of taste

Pré-salé (lit. salt meadow) is a term used in connection with the sheep which graze the ever-widening salt marshes of the southern Cotentin Peninsula; their numbers are most concentrated around the Bay of Mont Saint Michel. The grass which grows here is seasoned with sea salt and lends the meat of these animals a delicate and unique flavour. Pré-salé lamb has a well-deserved reputation in culinary circles and is served in every good restaurant in the region.

conceals a wonderful cheese which melts in the mouth.

Although crêpes are a Breton speciality, they are very popular here too, and made to equal perfection. The wafer-thin pancakes are served with a wide variety of fillings, both sweet and savoury, and every crêperie has its own special creation of which it is justifiably proud.

Normandy is famed for its patisserie. Apples and pears, of course, take centre stage. Traditional favourites include: *bourdelots*, apples stuffed with butter, sugar and cinnamon wrapped in pastry and baked; *douillons*, baked pears prepared in the same way; and, of course, the ubiquitous *tarte aux pommes*, that wonderful Normandy apple tart in its thin pastry case, served with crème fraîche and flambéed with Calvados – the crowning glory of any menu *à la normande*.

It goes without saying that none of these gourmet delights can be properly appreciated without a good drink. Normandy is not a wine-producing region and cider is the popular local drink. It is available everywhere, even in the top restaurants, and complements the regional cuisine extremely well. It is usually served dry, although sweet and medium dry ciders are available. The *cidre fermier*, which is packaged in champagne-style bottles, has the highest alcohol content and is of excellent quality, but it is priced accordingly. *Poiré*, or perry, is cider made from pears. It is less well known, but well worth trying.

Calvados, known locally as *calva*, is a rich, full-flavoured apple brandy. It is drunk before,

A secret blend of herbs and spices is used to make Bénédictine, the age-old liqueur distilled by monks

during and after a meal, and used liberally in cooking. You can even have a shot of Calvados in your cup of morning coffee (*café Calva*). The quality of Calvados is determined according to its age. It is graded from 3 stars (2 years), to *Réserve* (3 years), to VSOP or *Grande Réserve* (5 years). *Très Vieille Réserve* (6 years or more) is the highest category. The most sought after varieties are made in the Pays d'Auge; the fact that they are distilled twice earns them the AOC stamp of quality.

Popular aperitifs include *pommereau* (two-thirds cider and one third Calvados) and Bénédictine, a herbal liqueur distilled by the monks of Fécamp.

Camembert, Calvados and cider

*For fresh farm produce and other gourmet delights,
visit the local markets*

Normandy's economy is firmly rooted in the fruits of the land; its industrious farmers and fishermen have long benefited from its fertile pastures and well-stocked seas and rivers. The range of produce on offer is rich and varied, and the quality and presentation of the many local delicacies make them irresistible. Every town has its weekly market and strolling among the colourful stalls, listening to the chatter and immersing yourself in the bustling scene is one of the most enjoyable pleasures of any holiday in the region. This is where you'll find the the real farm-made charcuterie and cheese. A genuine camembert makes a nice gift for anyone who appreciates good cheese, but make sure it has the VCN (*Véritable Camembert Normand*) stamp of approval. Other names to look out for are Pont L'Evêque, Livarot, Brillat-Savarin, Neufchâtel and Pavé d'Auge.

Normandy has an inexhaustible range of souvenirs to offer: antiques, hand-made lace, copperware and gourmet food

Normandy is one of the few regions in France that does not produce wine. It does, however, produce top quality cider, the best of which is made in the Vallée d'Auge. *Cidre bouché*, which comes in bottles with a wired cork, is very popular, while *poiré*, pear cider, is a more unusual alternative. The best Calvados is made from Pays d'Auge cider and aged in casks. A good bottle is 2 to 3 years old; VSOP is at least 5 years old. Bénédictine, a liqueur made by the monks of Fécamp, is also a popular buy.

The local crafts can be expensive, but they make nice gifts: Villedieu-les-Poêles is renowned for its copper kitchen utensils; Alençon and Argentan produce beautiful lace; Rouen is famous for its faience. The numerous *marchands d'antiquités* throughout the region are a good source for gifts and souvenirs.

Most shops open from *08.30-12.30 and 14.00-19/19.30*, though there are no hard and fast rules. Some supermarkets stay open all day and often open on Sunday mornings, but may then close on Mondays instead.

Festivals and processions

From herring festivals to apple fairs, sailing and horse-racing

As is the case all over France, there is hardly a town or village in Normandy which does not have its own annual festival. These traditional events bring whole communities together and inevitably revolve around food and music. Considerable importance is also attached to religious and patriotic festivals. The national public holiday, Bastille Day, on 14 July, is one of the high points of the festive calendar in every region. Horse-racing in Deauville, the music festival in Honfleur, pilgrimages to Mont-Saint-Michel, the black-pudding fair in Mortagne-au-Perche, all attract big crowds. These events provide tourists with an opportunity to get a taste of the local culture and join in the celebrations. So the first port of call on arrival anywhere in the region should be the local tourist office (*Syndicat d'Initiative*) for details of festivals in the area.

Most shops and businesses close on *jours fériés* (public holidays)

The Medieval festival of Joan of Arc is held each May in Rouen

PUBLIC HOLIDAYS

1 January *(New Year's Day)*
Easter Monday
1 May *(May Day/Labour Day)*
8 May *(VE Day)*
Ascension Day
Whit Monday
★ 14 July *(Bastille Day)*
15 August *(Assumption of the Virgin)*
1 November *(All Saints' Day)*
11 November *(1918 Armistice Day)*
25 December *(Christmas Day)*

FESTIVALS & LOCAL EVENTS

February/March
Granville: Sunday before Lent, *Procession*

March
Mortagne-au-Perche: third weekend in March, *Foire au Boudin* (black-pudding fair)

April
Rouen: 30 April to 1 May, *International 24-hour motor boat race*, on the Seine

May
Coutances: first weekend in May, *Festival Jazz sous les Pommiers*

MARCO POLO SELECTION: FESTIVALS

1 Bastille Day
France's national holiday is a lively celebration in most towns (page 27)

2 Balloon festival
Every two years dedicated balloon enthusiasts from all over the world get together in Balleroy (page 28)

3 Horse parade
Throughbreds on show in the beautiful Haras du Pin stud (page 28)

4 Torchlit procession
The annual mass said for seafarers in Granville is atmospherically lit by blazing torches (page 28)

5 Polo and Grand Prix
Two major events in Deauville's busy social calendar (page 28)

6 St Nicholas market
The Foire Saint-Nicolas in Evreux fills the streets with Christmas spirit (page 29)

Cherbourg: *International sailing regatta*
Étretat: *Festival of the Sea*
Aigle: following Ascension Day, *The four days of Aigle*
Rouen: *Festival of Joan of Arc*
Honfleur: Whitsun, *Seamen's Festival* (blessing of the sea)
Bernay: Whit Monday, *Procession of the Hospitallers*
Beuvron-en-Auge: *Foire aux Géraniums* (geranium festival)

June

Le Havre: *International sailing regatta*
Deauville: *Horse-racing*
★ Balleroy: every other year on the second weekend in June, *International Balloon Festival*

July

Carrouges: *Concerts in the castle courtyard*
Deauville: *Jazz Festival* and *horse-racing*
Domfront: *Folklore Festival*
Fécamp: first weekend in July, *Festival of the Sea*
Le Havre: *International sailing regatta*
Honfleur: *Classical Music Festival*

La-Haye-de-Routot: 16 July, *Saint-Clair fireworks*
★ Granville: last Sunday in July, *holy mass for seamen* with torchlit procession
Camembert: last Sunday in July, *Fête de Camembert*

August

Livarot: first weekend in August, *Fête de Livarot*
Valognes: first week of August, *Festival of Music*
Barneville-Carteret: mid-August, *Festival of the Sea*
Sainte-Marguerite: second Sunday in August, *angling competition*
★ Deauville: end of August, *polo championships* and *horse auction*

September

Les Andelys: mid-September, *Foire à tout* (annual market)
★ Haras du Pin: first Sunday in September, *horse-racing, show* and *horse-drawn vehicle parade*
Lessay: 8-10 September *Foire Saint-Croix* (annual market)
Deauville: *Festival du Cinéma Américain* (film festival)

Avranches: third weekend in September, *Fête des Trois Quartiers*, (annual market)

Alençon: end September, *cattle market*

Mont-Saint-Michel: end of September, *Autumn pilgrimage in honour of the Archangel Michael*

Lisieux: third weekend in September, *Grandes Fêtes Thérésiennes*, (festival of St Thérèse), open day for all museums and historic monuments

October

Caen: *Tripes à la mode de Caen —* tripe competition

Pont d'Ouilly: *Foire de la Pomme*, (apple fair)

Le Pin-au-Haras: second Sunday in October, *Horse-racing* and *horse-drawn parade* at the National stud

Vimoutiers: third weekend in October, *Apple Fair* with processions

Vire: end of October, *Foie-gras annual market*

November

Vire: first weekend in November, *Sausage Fair*

Dieppe: third weekend in November, *Foire aux Harengs* (herring fair)

Beuvron-en-Auge: *Cider Festival*

St-Valéry-en-Caux: Annual herring market

Deauville: *Horse auction*

Alençon: last Sunday in November, *National Steeplechase*

December

★ Evreux: 6 December *Foire Saint-Nicolas*

A team of well-groomed cart horses on parade in Deauville

29

The Seine valley and the Alabaster Coast

*From ancient abbeys along the river banks
to the white chalk cliffs of the Côte d'Albâtre*

The Seine is a meandering river that winds its way in a series of broad curves and tight bends to the coast, widening as it goes. The boat journey from Vernon to Le Havre is 300 km long, whereas the same route by road is less than 150 km. Exploring this département by car is the better option, at least on a first visit. You will see much more of the variety it has to offer driving along its country roads and through the cobbled streets of its towns and villages. Historic and scenic treasures await discovery around every corner. Rouen has an endless array of beautiful and interesting sights, and the towns and villages around the capital are no less fascinating. When planning your drive through the valley, however, bear in mind that bridges across the wide expanse of water are few and far between.

The mouth of the Seine opens out at the port of Le Havre, at the beginning of the Côte d'Albâtre which runs eastwards as far as Le Tréport on the Picardy border.

The Gros-Horloge in Rouen has kept time for centuries

Hotel and restaurant prices

Hotels

Category L:	From 1000 FF
Category 1:	500–1000 FF
Category 2:	300–500 FF
Category 3:	up to 300 FF

Price per night for two people sharing a double room

Restaurants

Category L:	from 500 FF
Category 1:	300–500 FF
Category 2:	150–300 FF
Category 3:	up to 150 FF

Price per person for a three-course meal, excluding drinks

Abbreviations

FF	French Francs	**bd**	boulevard .
av	avenue	**pl**	place (square)

This is a rugged stretch of coast, lined with white chalk cliffs that are battered by choppy seas. They rise to heights of 200 m in places and are scored with deep indentations where the rivers have carved a course through the chalk plateau emerging into the sea. Dotted with little harbours, seaside resorts and a number of excellent beaches, the 'Alabaster Coast' has all the elements for an ideal holiday destination.

During the peak season, July and August especially, both the Val de Seine and Côte d'Albâtre are full of tourists. If you venture further inland, however, to the Pays de Bray, it is surprisingly quiet. This area is known for its production of cider (Longueville) and cheese (Neufchâtel-en-Bray). From busy, fashionable resorts to peaceful rural backwaters, historic monuments to seaside sports, the Seine-Maritime area has something for everyone.

DIEPPE

(G 2) Situated on the mouth of the River Arques, tucked between steep chalk cliffs, the port of Dieppe (pop. 40 000) still retains much of its medieval and distinctly Norman character. Its close links with Britain go back to the time of William the Conqueror who frequently used this port when he was king of England. During the French Revolution, aristocrats were smuggled across the Channel from here. By the mid-19th century, there were regular boat services between Brighton and Dieppe, which had become a fashionable resort for both French and British aristocracy. It was, in fact, the English who introduced the fashion for sea-bathing which had become all the rage. Dieppe's pretty sandy beach, which at low tide runs 2 km to the sea, is the nearest beach to Paris and is still a popular short-break destination for Parisians. Situated a little way from the town centre, its seafront promenade is lined with hotels of all categories.

Although it was one of the first seaside resorts, nowadays Dieppe is first and foremost a commercial centre. Its location predetermined its function as a safe harbour, and over the centuries it has developed into a major port for fishing boats, passenger ferries and cargo ships from all over the world.

SIGHTS

Castle

This sturdy medieval fortress, built to defend the town against the English, stands on a rock overlooking the seafront to the west of the town. The round tower dates from the 14th century and the rest of the castle was built up around it. The square tower was added in the 17th century. Dieppe was a major port of call for traders bringing ivory from Africa and India. At one time, there were around 300 ivory carvers living here. Among the many interesting exhibits in the castle museum are some intricate 16th-century ivory carvings.

Le Pollet

✪ The old fishing quarter on the right bank of the Arques with its crooked alleys and narrow flights of steps is a romantic place to explore on foot. The small church of *Notre-Dame-de-Grèves* has two beautiful frescos.

Les Tourelles

Of the original six town gates that were erected in the 14th century, only the 'Harbour Gate' has survived. It was used as a prison during the French Revolution.

Place du Puits Salé

★ This little square at the heart of the town is dominated by the *Café des Tribuneaux* — a fine 17th-century gabled building. In the 19th century the café was a popular haunt among artists and was frequented by the likes of Renoir, Monet, Sickert, Whistler and Pissarro. During his time in exile, Oscar Wilde was also a regular here. Not far from the café is the church of *Saint-Rémy* (16th/17th century) which features some interesting wooden panels.

Saint-Jacques

The magnificent church of Saint-Jacques (13th-16th century) is a mixture of Flamboyant-Gothic and Renaissance styles. Its square tower is 41 m high and there is a beautiful rosette above the portal. Also of interest is the *Chapel of the Holy Sepulchre* (15th century) near the entrance.

Musée du Château

High above the town, housed in the castle, is the civic museum. Alongside its valuable collection of ivory carvings are paintings by Renoir, Dufy and Braque.
Daily (except Tues) 10.00-12.00 and 14.00-17.00, Sun 14.00-18.00; Rue Chastes; Entrance: 13 FF

MARCO POLO SELECTION: SEINE-MARITIME

1 Rouen
The medieval old town is an architectural jewel (page 40, 41)

2 Fécamp
A long-established family resort, home of Bénédictine, the famous herb liqueur distilled by monks (page 38)

3 Étretat
Amazing rock formations sculpted by the waves rise majestically out of the sea (page 37)

4 Jumièges Abbey
The abbey church of Notre-Dame is one of Normandy's most impressive ruins (page 42)

5 On the scenic Route des Abbayes
The Château d'Orcher and Saint-Martin-de-Boscherville: two of the finest buildings in the Seine valley (page 38, 43)

6 Dieppe
The legendary Café des Tribuneaux overlooks the Place du Puits Salé and lends great atmosphere to this busy harbour town (page 33)

7 Le Tréport
The pleasures of a seaside resort below the high cliffs of the Côte d'Albâtre (page 34)

8 Varengeville-sur-Mer
Artists' village perched high up on the clifftops (page 35)

RESTAURANTS

La Marmite Dieppoise
Superb fish and shellfish dishes.
8 Rue Saint-Jean; Tel: 02 35 84 24 26; Category 2

La Mélie
Another excellent fish restaurant.
2 Grande Rue du Pollet; Tel: 02 35 84 21 19; Category 2

Le Panoramic
On the top floor of the La Présidence hotel, with views along the coast. Serves fine Norman cuisine.
1 Boulevard de Verdun; Tel: 02 35 84 31 31; Category 2

SHOPPING

⚜ The Saturday morning produce market in and around Grande Rue is definitely worth a visit. The stalls overflow with farm-made cheeses, pâtés, scallops, oysters, charcuterie, cider, fresh fruit and vegetables etc. Herring is an important local speciality and it even has a festival in its honour: the *Foire aux Harengs* is celebrated every year on the third weekend in November.

HOTELS

Aguado
A comfortable three-star hotel by the beach. Well-appointed rooms.
56 rooms; 30 Boulevard de Verdun; Tel: 02 35 84 27 00, Fax: 02 35 06 17 61; Category 2

La Présidence
A modern, well-run hotel by the beach. Offers thalassotherapy.
89 rooms; 1 Boulevard de Verdun; Tel: 02 35 84 31 31, Fax: 02 35 84 86 70; Category 1

SPORT & LEISURE

The riding and driving tournament in July and the horse-racing in August/September are the main annual sporting events.

INFORMATION

Office de Tourisme
Pont Jehan Ango, Quai du Carénage Tel: 02 35 84 11 77, Fax: 02 35 0 27 66

SURROUNDING AREA

Eu (H 1
Founded in 1151, this town (pop 5000) at the eastern end of the rocky coast is the oldest community in the region. ⚜ On plateau above the town stands the church of *Notre-Dame-et-Saint Laurent* (12th century), an impressive example of the Norman early Gothic style. At the centre of the town is the *Château d'Eu* (16th century) surrounded by gardens laid out in the classic French style. This Renaissance castle was King Louis-Philippe's favourite residence; he received Queen Victoria here twice. Also of interest is the chapel built in the style of Louis XIII for the former Jesuit College.

Le Pavillon de Joinville is a fine château hotel (*24 rooms; Route du Tréport; Tel: 02 35 50 52 52, Fax 02 35 50 27 37; Category 1-2*).

Le Tréport (H 1
★ This popular harbour town (pop. 6600) lies at the foot of high cliffs in beautiful surroundings Along with the neighbouring seaside resort of *Mers-les-Bains*, it has everything you need for a relaxing seaside holiday, including a

healthy climate. There are deep-sea fishing and sailing facilities along with open-air and indoor swimming pools. High above the town is the church of *Saint-Jacques* (16th century), worth a visit just to see its impressive Renaissance portal. A few kilometres further, on top of an even higher hill is the ☙ *Calvaire des Terrasses* observation point which offers a lovely panoramic view.

Nearby is the hotel/restaurant *La Vieille Ferme*, an old farm complex with a rustic atmosphere (*34 rooms; 23 Rue de la Mer, Mesnil-Val; Tel: 02 35 86 72 18, Fax: 02 35 86 12 67; Category 2*).

Miromesnil (G 2)

The Château de Miromesnil (16th/17th century) lies in picturesque grounds near Aubin-sur-Scie. Its most impressive feature is the elegant façade. The writer, Guy de Maupassant is believed to have been born here.
1 May-15 Oct, daily (except Tues) 14.00-18.00; Entrance: 30 FF

Varengeville-sur-Mer (G 2)

★ Perched high above the coastal cliffs and surrounded by hedges, this charming village has always attracted painters. The church which stands at the cliff's edge features a stained-glass window by Georges Braque entitled *The Tree of Jesse*. He is buried in the churchyard ☙ which has wonderful views over the coast and the cliffs. Also worth a visit is the 16th-century *Manoir d'Ango* (*daily 10.30-12.30 and 14.30-18.30; Entrance: 25 FF*). The gardens of the *Bois des Moutiers* are beautifully landscaped and ablaze with the colour of exotic flowers, at their best between April and June.

Church window by Georges Braque in Varengeville-sur-Mer

LE HAVRE

(**F 2**) This industrial city (pop. 250 000) on the north side of the 9 km-wide Seine estuary owes its existence to the silting-up of the ancient harbour of Harfleur. Founded in the 16th century it quickly developed into an important port. The city was razed to the ground during World War II, but it was painstakingly rebuilt from scratch and is now the second-largest seaport in France. The modern concrete buildings of the new town are purely functional and there are few sights worth seeing. Le Havre's one redeeming feature is its waterfront; it is an important sailing centre with a well-known marina, and has a good beach, *Sainte-Adresse*.

Espace Oscar Niemeyer

This impressive cultural centre, named after its Brazilian architect, is situated on the wide avenue which leads into the city. The complex includes a cinema, a theatre and exhibition halls. The *Bassin de Commerce* directly opposite is the site of Le Havre's international trade centre.

Hôtel de Ville

A short distance from the Espace Oscar Niemeyer is the *Place de l'Hôtel de Ville*, a spacious square dominated by the modern town hall and its 72 m-high tower. It is bounded by a park (*Jardin Public*), which has a monument to the French Resistance.

Notre-Dame

The chief attraction by the harbour is the restored cathedral of Notre Dame (16th/17th century), which displays a mixture of Gothic and Renaissance styles. Its four-sided bell-tower is quite a landmark. A notable feature of the interior is the organ, which was donated in 1638 by Cardinal Richelieu.

Port de Plaisance

⚓ One of the city's main attractions is the extensive Port de Plaisance marina which has over 1000 moorings. ◁ A fine view of the harbour can be seen from the *Mole Digue Nord*, a good place to go with your camera.

Sainte-Adresse

The north-western suburb of Le Havre is an elegant resort. ◁ The old town is built on a slope and there is a sweeping view from the neo-Gothic chapel of *Notre-Dame-des-Flots* which takes in the *Cap de la Hève* rocks and the old *Fort de Sainte-Adresse.*

Saint-Joseph

The modern concrete church of Saint-Joseph was built by Auguste Perret, the architect and town planner responsible for the reconstruction of Le Havre. It boasts a 106 m-high octagonal central tower and is punctuated by numerous small but brightly coloured stained-glass windows.

Musée de l'Ancien Havre

This museum, located in one of the oldest houses left standing in the city, has a wealth of old plans, documents and pictures illustrating the history of the port and city. *Daily (except Mon/Tues) 10.00-12.00 and 14.00-18.00; 1 Rue Jérôme-Bellarmato; Entrance: 10 FF*

Musée des Beaux-Arts André Malraux

Right by the harbour is the distinctive glass and steel building of the Museum of Fine Arts. The gallery's impressive collection of 19th- and 20th-century paintings includes works by Boudin, Corot, Dufy, Fantin-Latour, Monet and Pissarro.
Boulevard J F Kennedy

Musée du Prieuré de Graville

The priory church of Sainte-Honorine of Graville (11th century) features some beautiful capitals and also houses an interesting sculpture museum. *Daily (except Mon/Tues) 10.00-12.00 and 14.00-18.00; Rue Elysée-Reclus; Entrance: 10 FF*

RESTAURANT

Nossi Be
Restaurant with a pleasant atmosphere and inexpensive food.
50 Quai Féré; Tel: 02 35 42 77 44; Category 2

HOTELS

Clarine
Centrally located hotel.
86 rooms; Quai Colbert; Tel: 02 35 26 49 49, Fax: 02 35 25 10 13; Category 2

Ibis Le Havre Centre
Quiet, friendly hotel in the city centre.
86 rooms; Rue du 129ème Régiment d'Infanterie; Tel: 02 35 22 29 29, Fax: 02 35 21 00 00; Category 2

SPORT & LEISURE

🏊 During the summer season, Le Havre is a hive of seafaring activity, all of which is centred around the *Port de Plaisance*. The high point of the sailing calendar is the international regatta in June.

INFORMATION

Office de Tourisme
Place de l'Hôtel de Ville; Tel: 02 32 74 04 04, Fax: 02 35 42 38 39

SURROUNDING AREA

Cany-Barville (G 2)
This lively little town nestles in the picturesque Durdent river valley. It has an interesting town hall whose four wings enclose a large square. The main attraction, however, is the magnificent Château de Cany (17th century), 2 km south of the town. The castle grounds are laid out in the English style. Inside and out the magnificent building reflects the splendour of Louis XIII's reign (*daily, except Fri, 10.00-12.00 and 15.00-18.00 July-Aug; Entrance: 26 FF*).

Étretat (F 2)
★ This once quiet fishing village has developed into a lively and charming resort (pop. 1600), which attracts visitors all year round. People are drawn here by the beauty of the coastline and

The spectacular new Pont de Normandie which spans the Seine estuary, shortens journeys to the west of France

beach. ◁▷ To the west of the town is the *Falaise d'Aval* with views of the great cliffs, the 700 m-high Aiguille (the 'Needle') and the neighbouring rock arch, while to the east, the ◁▷ *Falaise d'Amont* offers a sweeping view over the resort and its spectacular rock formations. Other interesting sights in Étretat include the *Château des Aigues*, the church of *Notre-Dame* and the old town with its covered market hall.

A recommended restaurant here is *Le Bicorne* (*5 Boulevard René Coty; Tel: 02 35 29 62 22; Category 2*). A good hotel is *Le Donjon*, a lovely cliff-top manor house which offers fine views of the coast (*8 rooms, Chemin de St-Clair; Tel: 02 35 27 08 23, Fax: 02 35 29 92 24; Category 1*).

◁▷ If you are fascinated by strange rock formations, another stack worth seeing is the *Aiguille Belval*, 4 km further up the coast at Cap Antifer.

Fécamp   (F 2)

✦ Surrounded by beaches and cliffs, this long-established resort (pop. 25 000) enjoys a picturesque setting at the entrance to a valley in the Pays de Caux. Its popularity as a resort has been as enduring as its importance as a cod-fishing port. According to legend, a boat containing a few drops of Christ's blood landed here. The casket was later housed in the abbey church of *Sainte-Trinité* (12th century) making Fécamp into an important piligrimage centre. Across from the church stand the ruins of a palace (10th/11th century) once occupied by the dukes of Normandy. The old town is interesting to walk around, but the main attraction here is the *Musée de la*

Benedictine. The famous liqueur was originally distilled in this château from herbs gathered from the nearby cliff-tops. It has now been converted into a museum as the present distillery was moved to premises outside the town. The visit is rounded off with a glass of Benedictine (*daily 09.30-18.00; 110 Rue Alexandre-le-Grand; Entrance: 27 FF*).

Recommended restaurants in Fécamp include *l'Escalier* (*101 Quai Bérigny; Tel: 02 35 28 26 79; Category 2*) and *Le Vicomté* (*4 Rue Président Coty; Tel: 02 35 28 47 63; Category 3*). The *Hôtel d'Angleterre* also has a good restaurant (*32 rooms; 93 Rue de la Plage; Tel: 02 35 28 01 60, Fax: 02 35 28 62 95; Category 3*). A popular, comfortable hotel is the *Ferme de la Capelle* (*17 rooms; Côte de la Vierge; Tel: 02 35 29 12 19, Fax: 02 35 28 70 55; Category 2*).

Harfleur   (F 2)

❂ Harfleur (pop. 9700) was once an important harbour, but then it silted up and was superseded by the port of Le Havre 5 km east. It is, nevertheless, a popular destination for its colourful Sunday market. In the middle of the town stands the *Église Saint-Martin*, a five-aisled Gothic priory church (14th-16th century).

✦ ◁▷ Just 2 km from Harfleur, high above the Seine and surrounded by beautiful parkland, is the *Château d'Orcher* (18th century). This former defensive castle is dominated by a great crenellated watch-tower (*daily, except Thur, 08.00-17.00; Entrance: 20 FF*).

Veulettes-sur-Mer   (G 2)

This enchanting resort in the Pays de Caux at the mouth of the River

Durdent, boasts a marvellous seafront promenade. Further along the coast towards Dieppe are more pretty little resorts nestling by river estuaries. With their long stretches of sandy beach, places like Petites Dalles, Grandes Dalles, Saint-Valery-en-Caux, Veules-les-Roses, Sotteville, Sainte-Marguerite, Saint-Aubin-sur-Mer, Quiberville and Pourville are all ideal destinations for a seaside holiday.

Yvetot (G 2)

Following its near total destruction during World War II, little evidence remains of the former splendour of Yvetot, which was once capital of the ancient Pays de Caux kingdom. The pride of the town (pop 11 000) is now the modern church of *Saint-Pierre*, built in 1956, which has some magnificent stained glass. The *Musée du Pays de Caux*, a museum of agriculture and rural traditions, is worth a visit (*5 Mar-11 Nov, daily except Tues, 14.00-18.00; Entrance: 25 FF*). A good hotel is the *Hôtel du Havre* (*28 rooms; 2 Rue Guy de Maupassant; Tel: 02 35 95 16 77, Fax: 02 35 95 21 18; Category 2/3*).

ROUEN

(**G 3**) The importance of this city on the Seine is undisputed. With a population of around 120 000, it is the prosperous capital of both the département and the region. Its owes its commercial success to the Seine and its strategic position on one of the river's wide bends. Despite the fact that it lies 90 km inland, Rouen is the fifth-largest maritime port in France, and the busiest when it comes to agricultural exports. Each year, over 3500 ships dock here. The city's two thousand-year history has certainly been eventful. It was in Rouen that the Norman dukes resided and Joan of Arc was burned at the stake on the central *Place du Vieux-Marché*. Much of the ancient city was destroyed in World War II, but what remains of the medieval old town is well worth exploring. Wandering down the narrow streets and alleys there is still plenty of rich and varied architecture to admire. The magnificent sacred buildings, palaces and town houses that remain have earned Rouen the venerable title of 'Museum city'.

Wildlife

Once the region was covered in beautiful, wild deciduous woodland, the perfect habitat for a wide variety of fauna. As the woods were cleared over the centuries to make way for arable land, so the wildlife lost its natural habitat. Despite the decimation of the forests, however, wild deer still roam the countryside, and hares and wild rabbits thrive – much to the delight of the local farmers, most of whom are passionate hunters and can be seen every autumn stalking the stubble fields, rifle in hand. The fish stocks in the inland lakes and rivers are healthy, with plentiful trout, pike, whitefish and eels. It's no wonder that fishing is such a popular sport. Anglers from near and far come here to enjoy the abundant lakes and rivers and relax by their tranquil banks and shores.

Abbaye Saint-Ouen

This Benedictine abbey church (14th-16th century) is a magnificent Gothic building with a tall lantern tower in the Flamboyant style. The interior boasts some beautiful stained-glass windows (15th century) and a huge organ (16th century). On the north side are the ruins of the cloisters.

Mar-Oct, daily 10.00-12.30 and 14.00-18.00, Nov-Feb Weds, Sat and Sun only; Pl. du Général de Gaulle

Aître de Saint-Maclou

★ Behind the church of Saint-Maclou in *Rue Martainville*, a 16th-century cemetery lined with half-timbered houses lies hidden behind an unremarkable entrance that is easy to miss. The intricately carved galleries once served as a charnel house for the remains of the city's plague victims.

Daily, 08.00-20.00; 186, Rue Martainville

Beffroi and Gros-Horloge

★ The Gros-Horloge (16th century) is built into a Renaissance gate that spans the busy *Rue du Gros-Horloge*. The beautiful gilt clock still keeps perfect time. ☜ You can get a wonderful view of the city's spires, towers and half-timbered buildings from the top of the splendid *belfry* (14th century) just next to it.

Enquire at the Musée des Beaux Arts

Hôtel de Bourgthéroulde

The Renaissance colonnade of this stately Gothic palace (16th century) has some fine reliefs. *Place de la Pucelle*

Notre-Dame

★ The Gothic cathedral (12th-16th century) at the heart of the old town is considered to be one of the most beautiful sacred buildings in France. Monet certainly thought so: he painted it many times in different lights and at different times of year. Its majestic

The Palais de Justice in Rouen

façade is flanked by the *Tour de Saint-Roman* and the *Tour de Beurre* which was added later (16th century). This Flamboyant tower was financed by the 'butter (*beurre*) tax' paid by rich citizens in return for a special dispensation allowing them to eat butter during Lent. No less imposing is the iron spire, which at 152 m is the highest in France. The tombs of Rollo, the first Duke of Normandy, and Richard the Lionheart (which holds just his heart) can be found alongside other royal tombs in the crypt. Also of interest in the harmonious interior are the chapel dedicated to the Virgin Mary and the tombs of the Cardinals of Amboise. On weekends and summer nights the cathedral is beautifully floodlit.
Daily 08.00-19.00, Sun 08.00-18.00

Palais de Justice
The splendid law courts building (16th century) on the *Rue aux Juifs* is a classic example of the blending of Flamboyant Gothic and Renaissance styles. During its restoration, the remains of a 12th-century synagogue were found in the Cour d'Honneur.
Guided tours in summer Sun 11.00, the rest of the year Sat 14.00

Place du Vieux-Marché
★ The old market square is overlooked by half-timbered houses and the modern church of *Sainte Jeanne-d'Arc*. It was here, on 30 May 1431, that France's patron saint was burned at the stake. Her memory is honoured with a monument and the *Musée Jeanne d'Arc* opposite the church.
Daily 09.30-18.30, in winter 10.00-12.00 and 14.00-18.00; Entrance: 22 FF

Saint-Maclou
The *Rue Saint-Romain*, which is lined with some well preserved half-timbered houses, leads from the cathedral to the *Place Barthélémy*, the site of a late Gothic jewel: the church of *Saint-Maclou* (15th-16th century). Its magnificent porch is made up of five semicircular arches and displays a wealth of filigree ornamentation.
Daily 10.00-12.00 and 14.00-18.00

Musée des Beaux-Arts
The fine arts museum has a rich collection of 18th century masterpieces and a number of of Impressionist paintings by Claude Monet, Auguste Renoir and Alfred Sisley among others.
Daily (except Tues) 10.00-18.00; Square Verdrel; Entrance: 20 FF

Musée le Secq-des-Tournelles
The former church of St Laurent houses an exhibition of more than 14000 varied examples of wrought ironwork.
Daily (except Tues) 10.00-18.00; Rue Jacques-Villon; Entrance: 13 FF

Gill
The finest Norman specialities; try the *Pigeon à la rouennaise*.
9 Quai de la Bourse; Tel: 02 35 71 16 14; Category 1

La Couronne
France's oldest inn, housed in a magnificent half-timbered building. Both atmosphere and food are as good as you will find anywhere.
31 Place du Vieux-Marché; Tel: 02 35 71 40 90; Category 1

Les P'tits Parapluies

Restaurant in a 16th-century house furnished in Belle Epoque style. The food is equally refined.
46 Rue Bourg-l'Abbé; Tel: 02 35 88 55 26; Category 2

Les Quatre Saisons

The chefs in the Hôtel de Dieppe restaurant have perfected the art of traditional cuisine.
Place Bernard-Tissot; Tel: 02 35 71 96 00; Category 2

SHOPPING

Rouen is famous for its beautiful faïence, which can be bought all over the city. The best shops are found in the cathedral area.

HOTELS

Hôtel de Bordeaux

A friendly Inter-Hotel, near the cathedral.
48 rooms; 9 Place de la République; Tel: 02 35 71 93 58, Fax: 02 35 71 92 15; Category 2

Hôtel de Dieppe

A hotel with a pleasant atmosphere, located near the old town.
42 rooms; Place Bernard-Tissot; Tel: 02 35 71 96 00, Fax: 02 35 89 65 21; Category 1-2

Mercure Rouen Centre

A modern, beautifully appointed hotel, right in the heart of the city.
125 rooms; Rue Croix-de-Fer; Tel: 02 35 52 69 52, Fax: 02 35 89 41 46; Category 2

INFORMATION

Office de Tourisme

25 Place de la Cathédrale; Tel: 02 32 08 32 40, Fax: 02 32 08 32 44

SURROUNDING AREA

Caudebec-en-Caux   (G 2-3)

Life for the inhabitants of this small town (pop. 2700), surrounded by woodland on the north bank of the Seine, has for centuries been determined by the river's shipping traffic. Once an important port, it was badly damaged during the war, when the Germans set fire to it. Thankfully, the church of *Notre-Dame* (15th century), managed to escape destruction. Richly decorated in the Flamboyant style, it is a masterpiece of late Gothic architecture. Its 54 m spire is one of Normandy's architectural gems.

The lively history of the town is recounted through an audiovisual presentation and the pictorial displays in the *Musée de la Marine de Seine (daily 14.00-18.30; Entrance: 18 FF).*

Jumièges Abbey   (G 3)

★ The extensive ruins of this Benedictine abbey on the banks of the Seine are impressive indeed. Commissioned by Robert Champart, Archbishop of Canterbury, the abbey was consecrated in 1067 in a ceremony attended by William the Conqueror himself. The remains of the church of *Notre-Dame* dominated by the 43 m-high towers, give a good indication of the original size of the complex. The sections of the *Église Saint-Pierre* that are still standing, the remains of stone staircases, the chapterhouse and the cellar still reflect the beauty and splendour of Romanesque architecture. The ruins are visible from the river.
In summer daily 09.00-18.30; Entrance: 26 FF

The ruins of the Abbey of Jumièges still convey an air of the wealth and power they once possessed

Martainville (H 3)

The main attraction of this village east of Rouen, not far from Lyons forest, is the unusual *Château de Martainville* (15th century). It was originally built as a stronghold, hence the surrounding wall with its four corner towers and the ditch. The compact turreted castle is made of stone and brick and has some fine Gothic decorative features. It is now occupied by the *Musée départemental des Traditions et Arts Normands*, which houses an interesting collection of Norman furniture, costumes and household effects.

Daily (except Tues) 10.00-12.30 and 14.00-17.00; Entrance: 20 FF

Saint-Martin-de-Boscherville (G 3)

★ A peaceful locale, set in beautiful woodland. The nearby Romanesque abbey church of *Saint-Georges* is a large well-balanced structure with a simple porch and eight-bay nave. The semicircular arches of the 12th-century chapterhouse façade harmonize perfectly with the cloister.

Daily 09.00-12.00 and 14.00-17.00, in summer 09.00-19.00; Entrance: 25 FF

Saint-Maurice-d'Ételan (F 3)

The *Château d'Ételan* (15th century), set in picturesque grounds, is another fine example of Flamboyant Gothic architecture.

15 July-30 Aug, daily (except Tues) 14.30-18.30; Entrance: 20 FF

Saint-Wandrille-Rançon (G 2-3)

This Benedictine abbey nestling in the Seine valley was founded in the 7th century by Count Wandrille. According to legend, on their wedding day the count and his bride decided to sacrifice their love to God and became a monk and a nun. The abbey was largely destroyed during the Revolution. All that is left of the original buildings are the chapel of *Saint-Saturnin* (10th century) and some remains of the abbey church (13th-14th century). The current church building is a converted timber-framed tithe barn (15th century), brought here from the Eure and painstakingly re-erected piece by piece. The monastery buildings are inhabited and run by Benedictine monks. Their Gregorian chanting can be heard in the morning and evening.

Guided tours daily 15.00 and 16.00, Sunday also 11.30; Entrance 10 FF

River valleys and thick forests

Sleepy villages with their half-timbered houses are surrounded by meadows, woodlands, lakes and rivers

The route from Paris to the Côte Fleurie passes through the Eure. This département stretches eastwards from Calvados and Orne to just beyond the Seine. The wide open spaces of the western half contrast with the wooded landscape around the banks of the Seine. Apart from the Eure's most popular attractions — Giverny, Vernon, Gaillon and Les Andelys – there are plenty of other lesser-known sites worth seeking out. On the eastern side of the Seine the forest of Lyons is dotted with abbeys, hidden among the ancient oak and beech trees, while on the western side the broad fields of the Pays d'Ouche are interspersed with historic buildings. In terms of both nature and architecture, the département of Eure has plenty to offer.

EVREUX

(**G 4**) The capital (pop. 52 000) of the département, is an attractive and prosperous town set in the beautiful Pays d'Ouche countryside. In the past, fate has dealt the city some cruel blows; it suffered serious damage during the French Revolution and then again when it was bombarded during World War II. But each time it has faced destruction bravely and built itself back up. As a consequence of the successful rebuilding programme, Evreux has gradually developed into an important industrial and commercial centre, and with its numerous historic sights, it is now at the heart of a flourishing economic region.

SIGHTS

Couvent des Capucins
Near the *Jardin public* stands the old Capuchin monastery (17th century), a harmonious building whose beautiful cloisters should not be missed.

Notre-Dame
★ The ever-changing history of the city has always been inextricably linked with its cathedral. Over the centuries Notre-Dame has suffered damage and destruction, from when it was burned down in the early 12th century by Henry I to the severe damage

The cathedral of Notre-Dame in Evreux

45

inflicted on it during the German air raids in 1940. The impressive building is a mixture of styles dating from the 12th to the 17th century. The colourful stained-glass windows (16th century) are magnificent, as are the fine Renaissance gates of the choir chapel.
Daily 07.00-12.00 and 14.00-19.00

Palais Épiscopal

Connected to the cathedral by a cloister, the magnificent Bishop's Palace (15th century) now houses a museum.

Saint-Taurin

The *Promenade des Remparts* along the banks of the Iton river leads to the former abbey church of Saint-Taurin (10th-15th century) built over the grave of St Taurinus, the first bishop of the city. The famous 12th-century reliquary is an outstanding example of the goldsmith's art.
Daily 08.30-19.00

Tour de l'Horloge

Beyond the art gallery and the municipal theatre, opposite the town hall, stands the tall, slim, *belfry* (15th century). A 2-tonne bell hangs in the 44 m-high tower, which was rung to warn citizens of any impending danger.

Musée Municipal

This museum, housed in the Bishop's Palace, focuses on archaeology, but also has a fine collection of paintings. At its centre is a 60 m-long section of the original town walls.
Daily (except Mon) 10.00-12.00 and 14.00-18.00, Sun 14.00-18.00; Entrance free

L'Auberge de Parville

Friendly atmosphere and attentive service.
4 km out of town, RN 13; Tel: 02 32 39 36 63; Category 2

Le Français

Good Norman cuisine served in pleasant surroundings.
Place Clémenceau; Tel: 02 32 33 5. 60; Category 2

De France

Traditional establishment in the city centre.
16 rooms; 29 Rue Saint-Thomas; Tel 02 32 39 09 25, Fax: 02 32 38 38 56; Category 2

Normandy

Hotel with a warm atmosphere in a beautiful Norman half-timbered house.
25 rooms; 37 Rue Édouard Feray Tel: 02 32 33 14 40, Fax: 02 32 33 24 74; Category 2

Office de Tourisme

1 Place du Général de Gaulle; Tel: 02 32 24 04 43, Fax: 02 32 31 28 45

Anet   (G-H 4-5)

This little town lies on the banks of the Eure in the south-eastern corner of Normandy. Its star attraction is the Château d'Anet (16th century) which belonged to Diane de Poitiers, Duchess of Valentinois and mistress of Henri II. The well-preserved remains give a good idea of just how

MARCO POLO SELECTION: EURE

1 Evreux
The formidable Notre-Dame cathedral dominates the département capital (page 45)

2 Beaumesnil
Elegant château with exquisite sculptures, set in formal gardens. One of the finest examples of Louis III style (page 47)

3 Bernay
The abbey church is one of the oldest sacred buildings in Normandy (page 47)

4 Giverny
Monet's colourful gardens were a constant source of inspiration (page 49)

5 Les Andelys
Magnificent views from the citadel ruins (page 49)

plendid this Renaissance palace nust have been. Well worth a isit (*daily, except Tues, in summer 4.30-18.30, Sun also 09.00-12.00, t other times Sun and bank holidays 4.00-17.00; Entrance: 20 FF*).

A recommended restaurant erving excellent cuisine is the *luberge de Maître Corbeau (Place du Marché, Ezy-sur-Eure; Tel: 02 37 64 '3 29; Category 1-2).*

Beaumesnil (F 4)
★ This elegant Baroque château 17th century), complete with a noat, enjoys a magnificent park and setting and is comparable in grandeur to the châteaux of the Loire. Built in the Louis XIII tyle, its central wing is adorned with beautiful sculptures. The castle also houses a small museum that illustrates the art of bookbinding (*daily, except Tues, in ummer 10.00-12.00 and 14.00-18.00; Entrance: 35 FF*)

Beaumont-le-Roger (F-G 4)
The imposing ruins of the *Prieuré le la Trinité*, a 13th-century priory church just outside the village, ise above the picturesque Risle valley. In the village itself is the Renaissance church of *Saint-Nicolas* (13th-18th century) which has some fine stained-glass windows.

Bernay (F 4)
★ In the centre of this historic town (pop. 1500) with its half-timbered houses, stands one of the oldest churches in Normandy. The pure Romanesque *Église Abbatiale* (11th century) is striking for the beauty of its façades and arches (*daily, except Tues, in summer 10.00-12.00 and 14.00-19.00, in winter 10.00-12.00 and 14.00-17.30; Entrance: 8 FF*).

Le Moulin Fouret is a fine restaurant in a converted water-mill (*St-Aubin-le-Vertueux; Tel: 02 32 43 19 95; Category 2*).

Brionne (F 3)
This old town (pop. 5000) in the lush Risle valley was originally built as a fortress (11th/12th century). ◁▷ A fine view of the valley and woodland can be seen from the ruins of the *donjon*. If you want to stop here for the night, the nearby hotel *Le Logis* is a good place to stay (*12 rooms; 1 Place Saint-Denis; Tel: 02 32 44 81 73, Fax: 02 32 45 10 92; Category 2-3*).

Monet painted his lily pond in Giverny in all lights and seasons

Just 4 km from Brionne, set in woodlands, is the *Abbaye Le Bec-Hellouin* (11th century), which merits a detour. It was an important seat of Christian learning and Lanfranc and Anselm, two of its early abbots, both became Archbishop of Canterbury. Much of the monastic complex was destroyed during the Revolution but remains of the principal church, the *Saint Nicolas tower* (15th century), the chapterhouse and the cloisters (17th century) can still be seen.

The hotel/restaurant *Auberge de l'Abbaye* in a converted half-timbered house, serves hearty Norman cuisine (*10 rooms; Tel: 02 32 44 86 02, Fax: 02 32 46 32 23; Category 3*).

Conches-en-Ouche (G 4

Sitting on top of a spur, this charming little town (pop. 3500) dominates its stretch of the narrow Rouloir river. The focal point is the *donjon*, all that is left of what was once a mighty fortress (11th-12th century). The nearby church of *Sainte-Foy* is a pleasant surprise both for its unusual tower (18th century) and its 21 wonderful stained-glass windows. Dating from the 16th century, they depict scenes from the life of Christ and the life of the Virgin (*daily 08.00-18.30*).

Gaillon (G 4

The *Château de Gaillon* is perched on a rocky outcrop high above the Seine. Remains of the original fortress can be seen along with a Renaissance pavilion and gallery. *July-Aug daily (except Tues) 09.00-12.00 and 14.00-18.00; Entrance free*

Gisors (H 3-4)

The strategic importance of this town (pop. 9000) is clear from the well-preserved huge castle (11th century) which dates back to the times of the Norman Dukes. ◁▷ The observation point at the foot of the two *donjons* offers a far-reaching view across the town and surrounding countryside. The church of *Saint-Gervais-et-Saint-Protais* (13th-16th century) with its aisled choir and magnificent Renaissance portal, makes an interesting visit (*daily 08.30-18.00*).

Giverny (H 4)

★ Not far from the confluence of the river Epte and the Seine, lies the hamlet of Giverny, home of the great Impressionist painter, Claude Monet, who died here in 1926 at the age of 86. He designed and landscaped its wonderful garden which is, in itself, a work of art. The little Japanese bridge, the lily pond, and his vivid floral displays have all been immortalized in his paintings. The museum was acquired by the Academy of Fine Arts in 1966 and under their supervision the gardens are carefully tended and maintained exactly as Monet intended.
April-Oct, daily (except Mon) 10.00-18.00; Entrance: 35 FF

Harcourt (G 3-4)

Encircled by a 15 m-deep ditch and a wall with built-in watchtowers, the *Château d'Harcourt* (12th century) was well protected. The grounds of the medieval castle were planted with exotic trees, and the extensive forest beyond the estate boundaries is a good place to go for country walks.
Daily in summer 10.00-19.00, at other times daily (except Tues) 14.00-18.00, Entrance: 25 FF

Les Andelys (H 3-4)

★ ◁▷ Perched dramatically on top of a chalk cliff high above a picturesque loop of the Seine, the impressive ruins of the *Château Gaillard* dominate the peaceful town (pop. 10000) below. This citadel, commissioned by Richard the Lionheart in 1196, took less than two years to build. It was meant to block access along the Seine to Rouen and was an important bulwark of the Norman defences against the French. However, the stronghold fell to the French not long after. Then, in the early 17th century, Henri IV had the complex destroyed. The ruins, consisting of the keep surrounded by a defensive ditch

The ruins of Château Gaillard, sacked by Henri IV

49

and wall, are perfect photo-
graphic subjects, as is the expan-
sive view over the surrounding
countryside. (*15 Mar-15 Nov, daily
except Tues/Weds am, 09.00-12.00
and 14.00-18.00; Entrance: 18 FF*).

The former collegiate church
of *Notre Dame* (12th century) in
Les Andelys, with its lovely Renaissance portal, should not be
missed.

Lisors (H 3)

Nestling among the oaks and
beeches of *Lyons Forest* are the
ruins of the Cistercian Abbey of
Mortemer (12th century). There is
a small museum on monastic life
and a miniature train which takes
visitors on a tour of the grounds.
*Abbey: Easter-Sept 14.00-18.00, all
other times Sun 14.00-18.00*
*Park: open all year 09.00-13.00 and
14.00-18.30; Entrance: 35 FF*

Louviers (G 3)

This small town (pop. 20 000)
near the confluence of the Eure
and the Seine, is an important
centre for textiles. The church of
Notre-Dame (13th century) is a
fine example of Flamboyant
Gothic architecture. Of particular
interest are the richly orna-
mented portal and stained-glass
windows. Another unique building is the cloister of the *Couvent
des Pénitents* by the water. The
municipal museum houses an
eclectic collection of exhibits covering a wide range of subjects
and eras.
*Daily (except Tues) 10.00-12.00 and
14.00-18.00; Entrance: 10 FF*

Lyons-la-Forêt (H 3)

The centratl feature of this picturesque hill village (pop. 1000)
is the open market hall (15th century) where arts and crafts exhibitions are often staged. Renowned
for its restored timber houses
(17th/18th century), it is also the
main departure point for walking
and cycling tours in the surrounding countryside. The Lyons
Forest, thick with towering trees,
is criss-crossed with nature trails.
A wonderful place for the quiet
contemplation of unspoilt nature.

The charm of Vernon lies in its beautiful half-timbered buildings

In the Marco Polo Spirit

Marco Polo was the first true world traveller. He travelled with peaceful intentions forging links between the East and the West. His aim was to discover the world, and explore different cultures and environments without changing or disrupting them. He is an excellent role model for the 20th-century traveller. Wherever we travel we should show respect for other peoples and the natural world.

WWF

Pont-Audemer (F 3)

This sleepy little town on the banks of the Risle owes much of its charm to its picturesque streets and alleys lined with half-timbered houses (16th century). The churches of *Saint-Ouen* and *Saint-Germain* (both 11th century), dominate the centre. The town is a popular place from which to explore the marshlands of Vernier and forests of Brotonne.

Vascoeuil (H 3)

Designated a National Monument, the *Château de Vascoeuil* (12th century) and its 5 hectares of parkland have been made into an art centre. Paintings by contemporary artists are exhibited in the castle and dovecote, and modern sculptures are displayed in the park. *Daily 14.30-18.30, in summer 11.00-19.00; Entrance (includes castle and grounds): 40 FF*

Verneuil-sur-Avre (G 5)

This historic town (pop. 7000) on the Avre river has a number of pretty, well-preserved half-timbered buildings (15th/16th century). The 15th-century Benedictine church of *Saint-Nicolas* and the 12th-century Romanesque church of *Notre-Dame* are also of interest. ⚐ Lovely views of the town can be seen from the 60 m-high *Tour de la Madeleine*. You can

also see the *Parc Faugère* from here. It runs along the town wall and is a lovely place for a stroll.

Recommended hotel/restaurants: *Du Saumon (29 rooms; 89 Place de la Madeleine; Tel: 02 32 32 02 36, Fax: 02 32 37 55 80; Category 3); Le Clos (17 rooms; 98 Rue de la Ferté-Vidame; Tel: 02 32 32 21 81, Fax: 02 32 32 21 36; Category 3)* and the *Moulin de Balisne (10 rooms; Tel: 02 32 32 03 48, Fax: 02 32 60 11 22; Category 2).*

Vernon (H 4)

The focal point of this lively town (pop. 23 600) with its half-timbered houses, is the Gothic collegiate church. On the right bank of the river, near a romantic bridge, stand the ruins of a medieval château (13th century). This is also the location of the museum of local history, *Musée Alphonse-Georges Poulin (daily, except Mon, 14.00-17.30; 12 Rue du Pont; Entrance: 15 FF).*

On the edge of town is the splendid Italianate *Château de Bizy* (18th century). (*Museum: daily except Mon, in summer 10.00-12.00 and 14.00-18.00, weekends only in the rest of the year 14.00-17.00; Entrance: 34 FF*).

A good hotel/restaurant is the *Normandy (50 rooms; 1 Avenue Mendès-France; Tel: 02 32 51 97 97, Fax: 02 32 21 01 66; Category 2).*

The Norman Riviera and the Pays d'Auge

Beautiful châteaux, sandy beaches and lush pastures contrast with the inescapable reminders of war

The idyllic sandy beaches of the Calvados coast are an endless source of pleasure for those who like to spend their holidays by the sea. The Côte Fleurie, the 'coast of flowers', between Honfleur and Cabourg, boasts the exclusive resort of Deauville along with a string of more family-oriented resorts along the Corniche Normande. A little more modest, but equally good for beach holidays, are the seaside resorts of the Côte de Nacre. Since the Normandy invasion of 1944, these flat sandy beaches are referred to as the *Plages du Débarquement*; the Landing Beaches. The consequences of the Allied landings were far-reaching. Hardly a village or town escaped the long and violent battle which began the liberation of France and Europe. The numerous bunkers and war cemeteries in the area stand as constant, moving reminders of the death and destruction Normandy suffered.

Seafaring centre, commercial port, artists' colony and now tourist centre; the historic town of Honfleur is as busy and lively as ever

Since the war, however, the region has made an amazing recovery. The majority of war-damaged buildings have been restored, so that thankfully the architectural heritage of such historic places as Caen, Lisieux and Bayeux can still be admired.

Inland, the rich pastures of the Pays d'Auge are grazed by the black and white Normandy cows, prized for their meat and creamy milk from which all those exquisite cheeses and the distinctive Isigny butter are made. Between the meadows, vast apple orchards yield the fruit that makes the best Calvados and cider. This is the agricultural heart of the province.

BAYEUX

(**D 3**) The core of this historic town (pop. 16 000) on the Aure river has kept its original character completely intact. Unlike most other Norman towns, Bayeux survived the war unscathed. The magnificent cathedral that rises out of the huddle of buildings is a Gothic masterpiece. The medieval streets dotted with old townhouses, with slate roofs and copper gutters are the perfect place for a relaxing stroll. The town's other top attraction is, of course, the Bayeux Tapestry. Apart from giving a detailed pictorial account of the Norman Conquest, the miraculously well-preserved tapestry also conjures a vivid image of 11th-century life. The town gets pretty crowded in peak season, but thankfully the centre is now a traffic-free zone.

SIGHTS

Old town

Bayeux has the oldest half-timbered house in Normandy. Built in the 14th century, it overhangs the corner of the *Rue Saint-Martin/ Rue de Cuisiniers*. The *Rue Franche* is lined with medieval town-houses and the *Hôtel du Croissant* in the Rue Saint-Jean is another noteworthy building. The Aure bridge affords a lovely view of the watermill of *Croquevieille*. Nearby is the old fish market.

Notre-Dame

★ Bayeux's Notre-Dame cathedral is one of the oldest and finest Gothic cathedrals in France (11th century). Of the original Romanesque building, only the crypt and the core of the tower remain. The Gothic chancel was rebuilt in the 13th century, followed by the transept, the capitals of the side aisles and the central tower, whose Baroque top was added in the 19th century. The

MARCO POLO SELECTION: CALVADOS

1 Caen
A mixture of modern efficiency and historic beauty (page 57)

2 Côte Fleurie
Normandy's answer to the Côte d'Azur (page 64-66)

3 Deauville
An elegant seaside resort where you can chance your luck at the racecourse or roulette table (page 65)

4 Trouville
A pleasant, more down-to-earth resort than its neighbour across the river (page 64)

5 Honfleur
This romantic town, full of picturesque images, inspired many Impressionist painters (page 62)

6 Bayeux
The magnificent cathedral and tapestry must be seen (page 54)

7 Balleroy
This château is a superb example of the Louis XIII style (page 56)

8 Vaches Noires
Impressive rock formations carved out of dark brown cliffs (page 65)

9 Cabourg
Marcel Proust's favourite resort full of quiet Belle Époque character and charm (page 66)

10 Pointe du Hoc
A spectacular observation point on a stretch of coast renowned for its scenery (page 67)

walls of the central nave have some fascinating ornamentation.
Daily 08.00-12.30 and 14.30-19.00, in summer 08.00-19.00; Rue Bienvenue

Bayeux Tapestry

★ Known to the French as the *Tapisserie de la Reine Mathilde*, the Bayeux tapestry is invaluable both as a work of art and historical document. Originally embroidered to decorate the cathedral, the tapestry is now exhibited in the *Centre Guillaume le Conquérant*, an 18th-century building which was especially altered to accommodate it. The accompanying displays are interesting and informative, but the place does get very crowded in summer.
Daily 09.30-12.30 and 14.00-18.00; Rue Normand; Entrance: 37 FF (ticket valid for 4 museums)

MUSEUMS

Musée Baron Gérard

Housed in the old Bishop's Palace, next to the cathedral, this museum exhibits a mixed collection of paintings from the 16th to the 19th century along with a collection of Bayeux lace and some fine porcelain.
Daily 10.00-12.30 and 14.00-18.00, June-Sept 09.00-19.00; Place des Tribunaux; Entrance: 37 FF (ticket valid for 4 museums)

Musée Diocésain d'Art Religieux

An exhibition of sacred art, documents and manuscripts, and valuable gold artefacts.
Daily 10.00-12.30 and 14.00-18.00, in summer until 19.00; Hôtel du Doyen, 6 Rue Lambert-Leforestier; Entrance 37 FF (ticket valid for 4 museums)

Musée Mémorial de la Bataille de Normandie

War museum with documents, charts and film footage of the Normandy landings.
Daily 10.00-12.30 and 14.00-18.30, June-Aug 09.00-19.00; Boulevard Fabian-Ware; Entrance: 30 FF

Just across the road is the *British War Cemetery* with a simple yet moving memorial.

RESTAURANTS

Les Arcades

Delicious and reasonably priced fish and meat dishes.
10 Rue Latière; Tel: 02 31 92 72 79; Category 3

Le Baromètre

Restaurant in the lovely Château de Goville.
Le-Breuil-en-Bessin; Tel: 02 31 22 19 28; Category 1-2

SHOPPING

There are numerous craft workshops selling beautiful wood, ceramic and porcelain artefacts.
5-11 Place aux Pommes

HOTELS

Château de Goville

Luxury accommodation in a magnificent château, 11 km west of Bayeux.
9 rooms; Le-Breuil-en-Bessin; Tel: 02 31 22 19 28, Fax: 02 31 22 68 74; Category 1

Hôtel d'Argouges

A peaceful oasis near the historic town centre.
25 rooms; 21 Rue de Saint-Patrice; 02 31 92 88 86, Fax: 02 31 92 69 16; Category 2

In May the acres of orchards across the region are covered in white apple blossom

Le Lion d'Or

Lovely old coaching inn right in the town centre.

27 rooms; 71 rue Saint-Jean; Tel: 02 31 92 06 90; Category 1

ENTERTAINMENT

☀ The liveliest venues are the *La Queue du Chat* in Etreham and *Le Royal* in the Hôtel de Brunville.

INFORMATION

Office de Tourisme

Pont Saint-Jean; Tel: 02 31 92 16 26, Fax: 02 31 92 01 79

SURROUNDING AREA

Balleroy (D 3)

★ The 17th-century *Château de Balleroy* lies in the forest of Cérisy, about 20 km south-west of Bayeux. A long avenue leads up to the perfectly proportioned building, in a style reminiscent of the Italian Mannerist tradition. The ornamental gardens were landscaped by Le Nôtre who laid out the gardens at Versailles. The interior is sumptuously decorated and the *grand salon* has a fine painted ceiling (*Daily in summer, except Wed, 09.00-12.00 and 14.00-18.00; Entrance: 30 FF*).

The *Musée des Ballons* housed in the stable block focuses on the history and development of ballooning, something the château's last owner, the American tycoon Malcolm Forbes, was passionate about (*15 Mar-31 Oct daily, except Wed, 09.00-12.00 and 14.00-18.00; Entrance: 23 FF; castle and museum together 37 FF*).

Colombières (D 3)

This 15th-century château on the edge of the Aure marshes stands

within a medieval moated strong-hold. The main section is square and has a tower at each corner.
May-Oct daily 10.00-18.00; Entrance: 22 FF.

Creully (D 3)

Six days after D-Day, General Montgomery received Winston Churchill and George VI in the *Château de Creully* (11th-16th century). He set up his headquarters on the castle grounds, in the same military caravan he had used in North Africa. The BBC also set up a wartime base here. (*July-Aug daily 10.00-12.30 and 15.00-18.30; Entrance: 15 FF*).

Hotel/restaurant: *Château du Baffy*; 35 rooms; *Colombiers/Seulles*; Tel: 02 31 08 04 57, Fax: 02 31 08 08 29; Category 1

Saint-Gabriel-Brecy (D 3)

The *Prieuré Saint-Gabriel*, founded in the 11th century, was built and extended over the course of several centuries. Of interest here are the priory church and the prison tower (15th century). The former monastery complex now houses a horticultural college.
Daily 10.00-12.00 and 14.00-18.00; Entrance: free all year except July/ Aug 15 FF

Tour-en-Bessin (D 3)

This little village is dominated by the church with its elegant tower (13th century) and original chancel (15th century). On the northern edge of the village a long avenue leads to the small, pretty *Château de Vaulaville* (18th century), which has some wood-carvings, beautiful furniture and a collection of Bayeux porcelain.
Daily in summer, otherwise weekends only, 14.30-18.30; Entrance: 15 FF

CAEN

(**E 3**) ★ The former capital of the duchy of Normandy, once ruled by William the Conqueror, lies on a broad plain just 14 km from the sea. Caen (pop. 120 000) is the administrative centre of the Calvados département and an important industrial and cultural centre of the *Basse-Normandie region*. The University, founded in 1432, is one of the biggest in France. During the 1944 Allied invasion the city was almost completely destroyed. Fortunately, some of the historic buildings were spared, while others were painstakingly restored.

SIGHTS

Abbaye aux Dames

In the eastern part of the old town is the counterpart to the Abbaye aux Hommes, the equally magnificent Romanesque *Église de l'Abbaye aux Dames* (11th century), dedicated to *La Trinité*. It was founded by Matilda, William the Conqueror's queen, who is buried here. Its most interesting features include the crypt with its groined vaulting, the cloisters, and a French garden.
Guided tours daily 14.30 and 16.00; Pl. de la Reine Mathilde; Entrance: free

Abbaye aux Hommes

The best starting point for a round tour of the city is the *Place Louis-Guillouard* near the monumental Abbaye aux Hommes. The abbey church of *St-Etienne* was built in the 11th century in the Romanesque style by William the Conqueror who was originally buried here (during the Revolution, his tomb was ransacked and

his remains scattered). The abbey was extended two centuries later in the early Gothic style with turrets and flying buttresses. It is a masterpiece of sacred architecture. The abbey building, added to the church in the 18th century, has an impressive interior decor.
Guided tours daily 09.30-16.00; Entrance: 10 FF

Château

॥ The lively Rue Saint-Pierre, which has two particularly fine half-timbered houses, leads to the castle ramparts (11th century) built on a low rocky outcrop. Before the war the castle was surrounded by a cluster of medieval houses; now it is completely exposed. Two gates and numerous bastions are built into the castle walls which you can walk along and enjoy the view of the city skyline with its distinctive towers.

Hôtel d'Escoville

Opposite the church on the *Place Saint-Pierre* is the impressive Renaissance Hôtel d'Escoville, a 16th-century merchant's mansion. The lovely inner courtyard is decorated with sculptures.

Leroy Tower

The Leroy tower on the *Place Courtonne* was once a vital part of the city's defences.

Saint-Pierre

The 13th/14th-century Gothic church of *Saint-Pierre* stands on the *Place Saint-Pierre* at the foot of the castle walls. It features an impressive façade, numerous Flamboyant ornamental features and a 78 m-high Norman belltower.

MUSEUMS

Mémoriale Caen Normandie

The widely acclaimed *Musée pour la Paix* was opened by President Mitterrand in 1988. The story of France under occupation and the events of World War II are illustrated and analysed through evocative audio-visual displays and documentary films.
Daily 09.00-19.00; Esplanade Eisenhower; Entrance: 50 FF

Musée des Beaux-Arts

The Fine Arts museum houses an interesting collection of paintings by Italian and French masters (17th/18th century).

The floodlit city centre of Caen

Daily 09.30-12.30 and 14.00-18.00; Château ramparts; Entrance: 20 FF

Musée de Normandie

Also within the confines of the castle, housed in the former governor's quarters, this regional museum gives a comprehensive and informative view of the history of Normandy.
Daily 09.30-12.30 and 14.00-18.00; Esplanade du Château; Entrance: 10 FF

RESTAURANTS

Alcide

Traditional local cuisine.
1 Place Courtonne; Tel: 02 31 44 18 06; Category 3

Chantegrill

A good grill restaurant.
17 Place de la République; Tel: 02 31 85 23 64; Category 3

La Bourride

Top-class restaurant; excellent fish and meat specialities.
15 Rue de Vaugueux; Tel: 02 31 93 50 76; Category 1

SHOPPING

❧ Like most Norman towns and cities, Caen has a lively weekly market. You can find it on the *Place St-Sauveur* on Fridays and on the *Place Courtonne* on Sundays.

HOTELS

Le Dauphin

A good hotel, part of which was an old priory, with an excellent restaurant. Right in the city centre.
22 rooms; 29 Rue Gémare; Tel: 02 31 86 22 26, Fax: 02 31 86 35 14; Category 1

Moderne

Also in the centre. Breakfast is served on the 5th floor against a panoramic backdrop of the city.
40 rooms; 116 Boulevard du Maréchal-Leclerc; Tel: 02 31 86 04 23, Fax: 02 31 85 37 93; Category 2

INFORMATION

Office de Tourisme

Place St-Pierre; Tel: 02 31 86 27 65, Fax: 02 31 79 08 08

SURROUNDING AREA

Beuvron-en-Auge (E 3)

This historic village on the *Route du Cidre* in the heart of the Pays d'Auge, is under a conservation order. The market square is lined with an assortment of wonderful, half-timbered houses. One of the main attractions is the *Manoir* on the southern edge of the village.

Crèvecoeur-en-Auge (E 3)

An interesting fortified *Manoir* (11th-16th century) complex made up of several half-timbered buildings encircled by a moat. It is owned by the Schlumberger Foundation which has set up a small museum that focuses, rather incongruously, on petroleum.
April-Sept daily 13.00-19.00, at other times by arrangement; Tel: 02 31 63 02 45; Entrance: 27 FF

Falaise (E 4)

This little town (pop. 8500) in the bocage country was the birthplace of William the Conqueror. The story goes that his father, Duke Robert of Normandy, fell in love with a young girl named Arlette when he saw her washing clothes by a stream. When she fell pregnant, instead of going into confinement, she rode proudly through the castle gates for all to see and subsequently took up residence in the castle where she raised William. The *Fontaine d'Arlette* marks the spot where Robert first saw her. The view of the castle from here is quite lovely.

Falaise was of great strategic importance during World War II. It was the centre of the Germans' last stand in 1944 and as such suffered terrible damage. On seeing the town today, however, you'll find this quite hard to believe. The remains of the castle stand on an impressive rocky outcrop. The oldest part of the towering stronghold is the rectangular *donjon* (11th century). Parts of the town walls have been preserved, including a number of towers and gates, the finest of which is the *Porte des Cordeliers.* Below the gatehouse is the *Église Sainte-Trinité* (13th-16th century) which has many features typical of the transition period between the Gothic and Renaissance styles. Construction of the church of *Saint-Gervais* (12th-15th century) was begun in the Romanesque style and completed in the Gothic.

A recommended hotel here is the Château du Tertre (*9 rooms; Saint-Martin-de-Mieux; Tel: 02 31 90 01 04, Fax: 02 31 90 33 16; Category 1*).

Fontaine-Étoupefour (E 3)

Just outside the village stands the moated château of *Fontaine-Étoupefour*. A drawbridge leads to the entrance pavilion (15th century), which is decorated with pretty turrets, and beyond it lie the picturesque castle ruins (16th century).

Fontaine-Henry (E 3)

Built on the site of a 12th-century fortress, this large 15th-century château is set in an enchanting English-style park in the Mue valley. The interior decor is as appealing as the building itself. *Daily by appointment; Tel: 02 31 80 00 42; Entrance: 30 FF*

Lisieux (F 3)

The cathedral city of Lisieux (pop. 25 000) is the focal point of the Pays d'Auge and an important place of pilgrimage; the name of the town is inextricably linked with that of Sainte Thérèse who died here of tuberculosis in 1897, aged just 24. Each year the vast domed basilica of *Sainte-Thérèse* (1954) in the south-east of the town, welcomes thousands of pilgrims from all over the world (*daily 08.00-18.00, in summer until 20.00; Entrance: free*).

The Romanesque-Gothic twin towers of the 12th-century cathedral of *Saint-Pierre* show elements of all the various styles which influenced its architecture. Near the castle is the Bishop's Palace (17th century), worth seeing for the extravagant inner courtyard. There are some fine half-timbered houses in the old town.

Two of the best hotel/restaurants in the locality are the *Hôtel de l'Europe (24 rooms; 34 Rue de la Gare; Tel: 02 31 31 01 43, Fax: 02 31 31 27 27; Category 3)* and *La Coupe d'Or (18 rooms; 49 Rue Pont-Mortain; Tel: 02 31 31 16 84, Fax: 02 31 31 35 60; Category 3).*

Livarot (E 4)

This small town is best-known for its strong, full-flavoured cheese. Right in the heart of the Pays d'Auge, Livarot's attractions

The fairy-tale castle of Saint-Germain-de-Livet

include a number of manors and half-timbered houses, and the *Musée du Fromage de Livarot,* a cheese museum housed in the *Manoir de l'Isle (daily 10.00-12.00 and 14.00-18.00; Entrance: 12 FF).*

Mézidon-Canon (E 3)

Spread out along the Dives valley at the edge of the Pays d'Auge, this little town owes its historical importance to the *Château Canon* (18th-century). Built in the Italianate style, this grand mansion is surrounded by colourful flower gardens and shady avenues. *(Easter-30 Sept, daily except Tues, 14.00-19.00; Entrance: 25 FF).*

While in Mézidon, don't miss the beautifully restored *Breuil church* (12th century).

Pontécoulant (D 4)

Superbly located in the Durance valley, this château (16th/18th century) is one of the most impressive buildings in the Suisse Normande. Surrounded by an English park, the château houses the *Musée Départemental,* an interesting collection of furniture.

16 Apr-30 Sept, daily (except Mon) 10.00-12.00 and 14.30-18.00, 14.00-16.30 at other times; Entrance 10 FF

Saint-Germain-de-Livet (F 3)

This magical Renaissance castle lies in the Touques valley, 8 km south of Lisieux. The central wing built in the 14th century was extended in the 16th century with a Norman half-timbered house. The façade of the gatehouse with its slender *tourelles* is faced in brick and stone set in a chequer-board pattern. The inner courtyard is lined with Italianate arcades. The remains of frescos can be seen in the half-timbered wing.

Daily (except Tues) 10.00-12.00 and 14.00-17.00, in summer until 19.00; Entrance: 33 FF

Saint-Pierre-sur-Dives (E 3)

The focal point of this enchanting little place is its market hall built of sturdy Norman timber (11th/12th century). The building was destroyed in 1944, but it was carefully restored to its original form. A busy, colourful market is held here every Monday. The 11th-century Benedictine abbey church is one of the most beautiful Gothic buildings in Normandy.

Thury-Harcourt (D 3)

This little town (pop. 1700) is one of the gateways to the picturesque Suisse Normande area. The remains of the 17th-century *Château Harcourt*, which was burned down in 1944, lie on the banks of the Orne in a beautiful and colourful park laid out in the 18th century (*1 Mar-15 Nov daily 14.00-19.00*).

Vire (D 4)

A historic town (pop. 16 000) in the south-western *Bocage Virois* region. Sights of interest include the remains of a 13th-century castle keep, the *Porte Horloge*, the church of *Notre-Dame* and the watch-towers of *Saint-Sauveur* and *Raines*. Perched high up on a rocky outcrop are the ruins of an ancient fortress (12th century) with a square *donjon*. ⬂ The view over the Vire valley and

gorges is splendid. Vire is also famous for its *Andouille de Vire*, a traditional smoked sausage.

A recommended hotel is the *Hôtel de France* (*20 rooms; 4 Rue d'Aignaux; Tel: 02 31 68 00 35, Fax 02 31 68 22 65; Category 2-3*).

HONFLEUR

(F 3) ★ By far the most beautiful port on the Norman coast, Honfleur (pop. 8600) benefits from a prime location on the Seine estuary. Among the many great explorers to set sail from here was Samuel de Champlain, founder of the French colony of Quebec (1608). When the harbour was expanded in the 17th century trade blossomed, and the industrious fishing port became an important centre of commerce. One of the town's leading lights in the 19th century was the Impressionist Eugène Boudin, whose Saint-Siméon school attracted an increasing number of painters including Monet, Sisley, Pissarro and Cézanne, and the town grew into a veritable artists' colony.

SIGHTS

Lieutenance

The grand stone buildings of the Lieutenance (16th/17th century) the remains of the old fortifications, stand guard over the end of the harbour basin. This former seat of the royal governor now houses the offices of the port authority. The lock at the side of the building enables boats to put out to sea at low tide.

Mont Joli

A winding road to the west of the town leads to the chapel of

Notre-Dame-de-Grâce (17th century) with its slate-roofed tower. ✍ From the square in front of this pilgrimage chapel there is a wonderful panoramic view of Honfleur, the Seine estuary and the bridge of Tancarville.

Old town

In the romantic *Sainte-Catherine* district the cosy streets and alleys are lined with half-timbered houses. It is a beautiful area to explore and attracts streams of tourists. Look out for the two 17th-century *salt stores* in the *Rue de la Ville*.

Sainte-Catherine

The impressive wooden church of *Sainte-Catherine* (15th century) is a remarkable structure that dominates the *Place Sainte-Catherine* in the old town. Among its many unusual features are two parallel naves and a freestanding belfry clad in chestnut weatherboarding.
Daily (except Tues) 10.00-12.00 and 14.00-18.00

Saint-Étienne

The port's oldest church (14th century) and the focal point of the *Quai Saint-Étienne*.

Vieux Bassin

Honfleur's picturesque centrepiece is the old harbour basin (17th century) with its colourful yachts and fishing boats. ✍ A chocolate-box scene of tall, narrow, slate-clad houses with bars and cafés on the ground floors lines the *Quai Sainte-Catherine*. These delightful surroundings, once frequented and painted by great artists, today attracts mostly photographers.

Musée de la Marine

The maritime museum documents the history of the seafaring explorers who set sail from here.
Église Saint-Étienne; in summer daily, otherwise weekends only 10.30-12.00 and 14.30-18.00; Entrance: 25 FF

Musée Eugène Boudin

Exhibits a selection of paintings by the artist, alongside the rather superior works of Dufy, Monet and Courbet among others. Also has a good collection of Norman traditional costumes.
Place Erik-Satie; 15 Mar-30 Sept daily (except Tues) 10.00-12.00 and 14.00-17.00, at other times 14.30-17.00; Entrance: 18 FF

L'Absinthe

Delicious fish and seafood dishes right by the harbour.
10 Quai de la Quarantaine; Tel: 02 31 89 39 00; Category 2

Le Belvédère

Excellent restaurant with a traditional Norman menu.
36 Rue Emile-Rénouf; Tel: 02 31 89 08 13; Category 2

For such a small town, Honfleur has a lot of commercial galleries.

Ferme Saint-Siméon

This former artists' haunt is today a luxury inn with restaurant.
34 rooms; Rue Adolphe-Marais; Tel: 02 31 89 23 61, Fax: 02 31 89 48 48; Category L

Hostellerie Lechat

A grand old hotel/restaurant in the town centre.
23 rooms; Place Sainte-Catherine; Tel: 02 31 89 23 85, Fax: 02 31 89 28 61; Category 1

Hotel de la Tour

Well-appointed, friendly hotel nicely located near the harbour.
48 rooms; 3 Quai de la Tour; Tel: 02 31 89 21 22, Fax: 02 31 89 53 51; Category 2

ENTERTAINMENT

The *Vieux Bassin* and nearby picturesque squares are pretty lively in the evenings. As Honfleur is such a busy tourist centre, there is no shortage of bars or restaurants. If all this is not quite loud enough for you, you can always go on to the *Black Jack* disco on the *Route Jean Revel*.

INFORMATION

Office de Tourisme

Rue de la Ville; Tel: 02 31 89 23 30, Fax: 02 31 89 31 82

ALONG THE CÔTE FLEURIE

Trouville   (F 3)

★ Trouville (pop. 6500) may not be as sophisticated as its sister resort, Deauville, on the other side of the river, but it does possess a certain charm. The former fishing village has been a seaside resort since the 19th century. It has an extensive sandy beach and the promenade is lined with some magnificent villas. The town museum in the *Villa Montebello* (*daily 10.00-12.00 and 14.00-19.00; Entrance: 10 FF*) and the *Aquarium écologique* (*daily 10.00-12.00 and 14.00-19.00, in summer 10.00-19.30; Entrance: 30 FF*) are interesting places to visit,

Deauville's most sophisticated 'habitués' stay at the Hotel Normandy

64

and a stroll around the bustling fish market is an agreeable way to spend a morning. If you have some spare cash to fritter away, a fun place to go in the evening is the *Le Louisiane Follies* casino.

Recommended hotel/restaurants: *Le Clos Saint-Gatien*, a hotel in the *Château St-Gatien-de-Bois* (*53 rooms; Tel: 02 31 65 16 08; Category 1*), the *Mercure* (*80 rooms; Place Foch; Tel: 02 31 87 38 38; Category 1*) and the *Relais de la Cahotte* (*32 rooms; 11 Rue Victor Hugo; Tel: 02 31 98 30 20; Category 2*).

Deauville (E 3)

★ Deauville (pop. 5000), once a bastion of aristocratic high society, draws hordes of tourists in season and has lost something of its exclusivity, though with its famous casino, luxury hotels, yacht marina, racecourse, designer boutiques and Rolls-Royces carelessly parked along the promenade, it obviously still draws a well-heeled crowd. The names of long-departed stars and starlets inscribed on the beach huts and admired by the tourists give the place an air of faded glamour. The resort is now concentrating on its new image as a conference venue. There is a wide range of activities on offer, from horse-racing and polo to golf and sailing, and the wide sandy beach is excellent for bathing. In the evenings, the casino not only offers roulette and Black Jack but also stages plays and shows. Other entertainment venues include three night clubs and numerous discos.

Two of the more refined restaurants are *Le Ciro's* (*Promenade des Blanches; Category 1*) and *Le Spinnaker* (*52 Rue Mirabeau; Category 1*). The *Ibis* is a pleasant, affordable hotel (*95 rooms; 9 Quai de la Marine; Tel: 02 31 98 38 90, Fax: 02 31 98 38 36; Category 2*); while the *Normandy* is top of the range — a legendary luxury hotel steeped in tradition (*300 rooms; 38 Rue Jean-Mermoz; Tel: 02 31 98 66 22, Fax: 02 31 98 66 23; Category L*).

Villers-sur-Mer (E 3)

This classic resort faces on to a 5 km fine sandy beach (good for children) and boasts a number of romantic 19th-century half-timbered houses. The *Musée paléontologique* has an interesting collection of fossils found in the cliffs of the surrounding area (*daily 10.00-12.30 and 14.00-19.00; Entrance: free*).

Vaches Noires (E 3)

★ Known as the 'black cows', these dark, rugged marl cliffs have some impressive shapes. You can admire them from the beach beneath, accessible via a footpath from Auberville.

Houlgate (E 3)

This traditional French seaside resort has been a popular holiday spot for generations. Fine views of the coast and the Dives estuary can be seen from the nearby clifftops.

A central, comfortable hotel is the *Du Centre* (*22 rooms; 31 Rue des Bains; Tel: 02 31 24 80 40, Fax: 02 31 28 52 21; Category 2*).

Dives-sur-Mer (E 3)

It was from the ancient port of Dives (pop. 6000) that William the Conqueror set off with his 3000-strong fleet for Hastings and the conquest of England. The port is now silted up, but the 15th-century wooden market hall is still standing as are a number of old 16th-century houses and the Romanesque church of *Notre-Dame* (11th-15th century). The elegant shops of the *Village d'Art Guillaume-le-Conquérant,* specialize in art, crafts and antiques.

Cabourg (E 3)

★ Cabourg was designed in 1860 as a purpose-built holiday resort. All the streets radiate out in straight lines from the casino and are lined with charming *Belle Époque* houses. The *Promenade Marcel Proust,* which runs along the edge of the sandy beach, was named after the great writer who came here to benefit from the coastal climate and was a frequent guest at the *Grand Hotel.* The romantic resort (pop. 3000) offers plenty of leisure amenities which include a yacht club, sailing schools, sailboarding and other water-sport facilities. The night-life is centred around the casino which, apart from the gambling arena, has a theatre, cinema, nightclub and several bars.

Merville-Franceville (E 3)

The most westerly resort on the *Côte Fleurie* lies on the edge of the sandy Orne estuary. The *Redoute de Vauban,* an 18th-century fortress, was used by the Germans as part of their defences against the 1944 Allied invasions. Documents on display in the *Casemate No 1* tell the story of those fateful events.

ALONG THE CÔTE DE NACRE

Ouistreham-Riva-Bella (E 3)

The harbour town of Ouistreham (pop. 6000) at the mouth of the Orne, 41 km from Bayeux, is now a major ferry port used mostly by Brittany Ferries who run a regular service between here and Portsmouth. Sights of interest in the town include the Romanesque church of *Saint-Samson* (12th century) and the 15th-century stone tithe barn. *Riva-Bella,* now merged with Ouistreham, is one of the most popular beach resorts on the Côte de Nacre which begins here. Information: *Côte de Nacre Tourisme, 25 Rue E Belin, 14730 Lion-sur-Mer; Tel: 02 31 96 43 55.*

A recommended hotel/restaurant is the *Broche d'Argent (Place Général-de-Gaulle; Tel: 02 31 97 12 16, Fax: 02 31 97 03 33; Category 2).*

A trip to the nearby *Château Bénouville* (18th century) set in extensive parkland by the river Orne is a pleasant inland excursion.

Courseulles-sur-Mer (E 3)

The coast road from *Riva-Bella* leads from one resort to the next. *Lion-sur-Mer, Luc-sur-Mer, Langrune-sur-Mer, Saint-Aubin-sur-Mer* and *Courseulles-sur-Mer* all have the advantage of wide sandy beaches, perfect for sunbathing, swimming and relaxing *en famille.* Courseulles and its former fishing harbour are popular destinations for yachts and boats, not least because of the famed oysters cultivated here.

A recommended hotel/restaurant is the *Ferme de la Rançonnière (35 rooms; Crépon, Route d'Arromanches; Tel: 02 31 22 21 73, Fax: 02 31 22 98 39; Category 2-3).*

Arromanches-les-Bains (D 2-3)

This small, peaceful fishing port was one of the central landing sites for the Allied invasion of 1944. One of the prefabricated

Houlgate is a traditional family resort

Mulberry harbours which was towed in sections from England, was set up here, remnants of which can still be seen offshore. Along with a number of floating pontoons, it provided a secure landing for two and a half million troops and thousands of tonnes of artillery, along with supplies for the military operations which were to follow. An informative exhibition in the *Musée du Débarquement* on the main square describes the operations in detail. *Daily (except Mon) 09.00-11.30 and 14.00-17.30; Entrance: 32 FF*

Omaha Beach (D 2)

On 6 June 1944, the eastern section of the Côte de Nacre, divided into *Sword Beach*, *Juno Beach* and *Gold Beach*, was where the English and Canadian troops came ashore. The American troops landed at *Omaha* and *Utah Beach* to the west; theirs was the most costly operation. The landings were hampered by rough seas and strong currents and they suffered heavy casualties. The area is scattered with war cemeteries and museums, monuments and plaques, and the remains of the massive bunkers and defences.

Today, the wide sandy beaches are popular with windsurfers, due to the prevailing winds at low tide.

Pointe du Hoc (D 2)

★ Just before Grandcamp-Maisy, the most westerly place on the Côte de Nacre (renowned for its scallops) is the *Pointe du Hoc*, one of the most spectacular features on this stretch of coast. The rocky promontory was of strategic importance and the scene of intense fighting during the Normandy landings. The remains of bunkers, gun emplacements, and holes left by shells are poignant reminders of the horrors of war.

67

Around the Cotentin Peninsula

Where pastoral Normandy meets wild Brittany

The département of Manche marks the transition between Normandy and Brittany, and its landscape is an interesting combination of wild and tamed nature. The region is dominated by the Cotentin Peninsula with its broad meadows and fine beaches sheltered beneath high cliffs that line the windlashed shores. The bare, thin soil of the peninsula supports little more than grass pastures, surrounded by hedges. Sprawling moors are carpeted with a variety of bushes and shrubs which bloom prolifically in summer; thick forests cover other parts of the thinly populated interior. The north coast of the peninsula is wild, rugged and bracing, while the shores of the east and west coasts are lined with wide expanses of sandy beach. The only drawback is that the ebb tide draws the sea a long way out, which is causing the Baie du Mont Saint Michel gradually to silt up; a problematic situation for the monastery island. One com-

pensation is that the salt meadows are expanding. The meat from the cows and sheep that graze on the *prés-salés* has a unique aromatic flavour much prized by gourmets. Agriculture, especially dairy farming, is vital to the local economy; apart from the tourist trade there are few other ways of making a living here.

AVRANCHES

(C 4) The unique position of this historic town on a granite outcrop overlooking the *Baie du Mont Saint Michel* has been an important factor in its development. The Bishop of Avranches founded the original Benedictine abbey dedicated to the Archangel Michael on the island then known as Mont Tombe. Avranches has maintained close links with the Mont-St-Michel ever since. The bustling old town with its beautiful old buildings and medieval alleys is an interesting place to explore on foot. The fertile surroundings have made the ancient cathedral city (pop. 8700) into an important agricultural centre for a region which is largely dependent on sheep farming.

Floral displays in the Jardin des Plantes in Avranches, the former garden of a Capuchin monastery

Donjon

The remains of the old castle fortifications are dominated by the 13th-century keep which was heavily defended by battlements and machicolations. Beyond the tower is a square, the site of the former cathedral which fell to ruin in 1794. The stone platform here marks the spot where, in 1172, Henry II of England publicly repented for the murder of Thomas-à-Becket by his knights.

Jardin des Plantes

★ ↔ These beautifully tended botanical gardens were once part of a Capuchin monastery. There is a fine view of the *Mont-Saint-Michel* from the terrace.

Patton Memorial

This memorial garden, made with earth brought here from various US states, is officially American territory. The monument commemorates the first attack against the Germans that was launched from here by General Patton.

Saint-Gervais

This basilica, with its 74 m-high granite tower, is the town's most prominent landmark. The *Musée du Trésor de la Basilique St-Gervais*, within the church, houses a display of valuable treasures including an ancient reliquary.
Daily (except Tues) 10.00-12.00 and 14.00-18.00; Entrance: 12 FF

Bibliothèque du Fonds Ancien

Displays a precious collection of medieval manuscripts from the Mont-Saint-Michel.
June-Aug daily (except Tues) 10.00-12.00 and 14.00-18.00; in the town hall; Entrance: 20 FF

MARCO POLO SELECTION - MANCHE

1 Mont-Saint-Michel
One of Europe's greatest sacred buildings (page 77)

2 Barfleur
A picturesque fishing port on the north-east tip of the Cotentin peninsula (page 75)

3 Martinvast
A fine Norman castle set in a pretty park filled with lakes and fountains (page 75)

4 Sainte-Mère-Église
The parish church is crowned with an unusual memorial to an American paratrooper (page 76)

5 St-Vaast-la-Hougue
Some of the best oysters in France are produced here (page 76)

6 Haras National
Founded by Napoleon I, the national stud is renowned for its world-class thoroughbreds (page 79)

7 Abbaye Saint-Trinité
Benedictine monastery in a beautiful moorland setting (page 81)

8 Avranches
Wonderful views of the Mont-Saint-Michel from the botanical gardens (page 70)

Most of the inhabitants of Grande Île in the Chausey Islands are fishermen

Musée Municipal

The former Bishop's Palace now houses the municipal museum. The most interesting exhibit here is the collection of beautiful illuminated manuscripts (8th-15th century), the majority of which were written by monks in the Mont-Saint-Michel abbey.

April-Sept daily (except Tues) 10.00-12.00 and 14.00-18.00; Place Jean de Saint-Avit; Entrance: 12 FF

RESTAURANT

Jardin des Plantes

Simple home-cooking in pleasant surroundings. Good value. Also a reasonable hotel.

10 Place Carnot; Tel: 02 33 58 03 68; Category 2

HOTEL

Les Abrincates

Stylish hotel.

29 rooms; 37 Boulevard du Luxembourg; Tel: 02 33 58 66 64, Fax: 02 33 58 40 11; Category 2-3

INFORMATION

Office de Tourisme

2 Rue du Général de Gaulle; Tel: 02 33 58 00 22, Fax: 02 33 68 13 29

SURROUNDING AREA

Ducey   (C 4)

A tour of the *Sélune valley*, which cuts deep into the granite rock, makes an interesting excursion. The best place to start is the little town of Ducey. The river crossing was of strategic importance back in Roman times and a castle was subsequently built to defend it. Two lakes have been formed by the dams at *La Roche-qui-Boit* and *Vézins*, both of which offer excellent water sports facilities. The Sélune valley river is ideal for both canoeing and fishing.

Granville   (B 3)

This popular resort (pop. 15 600) is perched on top of a rocky outcrop which reaches far out into the bay of *Mont-Saint-Michel*. The greatest tidal variations in Europe which can reach up to 14 m, are recorded here. On the ridge of the rock surrounded by a defensive wall is the imposing granite citadel of *Haute Ville*. Of interest in the old town is the church of *Notre Dame* (15th-17th century) and the fortified town gate, the *Grande Porte*; it houses the *Musée du Vieux Granville* (*daily, except Tues, 10.00-12.00 and 14.00-18.00; 2 Rue Lecarpentier; Entrance: 10 FF*) which focuses on regional and local history. The narrow streets run past numerous old town houses (16th-18th century). A walk around the town walls yields fine views over harbour, coast and sea. The walk along the cliff path to the *Pointe du Roc* and its lighthouse is beautiful.

Basse Ville, the ferryport and fishing harbour area, has a number of restaurants specializing in fresh seafood. One of the best is *Le Phare* (*11 Rue Port; Tel: 02 33 50 12 94; Category 2*). The choice of hotels includes *Des Bains* (*49 rooms; 19 Rue Clémenceau; Tel: 02 33 50 17 31, Fax: 02 33 50 89 22; Category 1-2*) and *Le Herel* (*43 rooms; Port de Plaisance; Tel: 02 33 90 48 08, Fax: 02 33 90 75 95; Category 2*).

Îles Chausey (B 3)

The Chausey Islands lie off the west Cotentin coast. At high tide there are 50 islands, while at low tide the number increases to 350. The largest island in the archipelago, *Grande Île*, is the only one which is populated, and most of

St-Vaast-la-Hougue: a popular port of call with cross-Channel yachts

72

its inhabitants are fishermen. The coastal waters around the islands are well stocked with lobsters and crabs. Granite used to build the Mont-St-Michel was quarried on these islands. A boat service to the Îles Chausey operates in summer from Granville and the journey takes about an hour.

Mortain (C 4)

Spread across a low hill, Mortain (pop. 3000) is surrounded by the enchanting landscape of the *Bocage Mortainais*. The town, which has been fortified since Norman times, has a 12th-century Cistercian abbey, the *Abbaye Blanche*, now a spiritual retreat. Sites of interest include the church, chapterhouse, cellars and remains of a Romanesque cloister with lovely semicircular arches (*June-Sept daily, except Tues, 09.15-12.00 and 14.30-17.30*). As you leave the historic town and proceed through the *Cance Valley* you will come to the *Grande Cascade*, a waterfall which drops 25 m, hidden away in a wilderness of granite boulders. Nearby is the 35 m high *Petite Cascade* — a longer but less spectacular drop.

Villedieu-les-Poêles (C 4)

This little town (pop. 5000) in the heart of 'bocage' country was founded in the 11th century by the Order of the Knights of St John. It lies in the *Sienne valley*, which is famed for its trout. The town itself, whose name means something like 'god's frying pan town', is renowned for its coppersmiths and bell founders. The bell foundry is open to visitors, as are the numerous copper workshops which turn out all sorts of pots and pans and copper utensils.

(Fonderie de Cloches Atelier Cormille-Havard: Rue du Pont Chignon; daily 08.00-12.00 and 14.00-17.30. Atelier du Cuivre: 54 Rue du Général Huard; daily 09.00-12.00 and 14.00-18.30).

The 15th-century stone church of *Notre-Dame*, built in the Flamboyant Gothic style, features a square transept tower topped by a lantern dome.

The best hotels include the *Manoir de l'Acherie (14 rooms; Sainte-Cécile; Tel: 02 33 51 13 87, Fax: 02 33 61 89 07; Category 2-3)* and the *Saint-Pierre et Saint-Michel (23 rooms; 12 Place de la République; Tel: 02 33 61 00 11, Fax: 02 33 61 06 52; Category 2).*

CHERBOURG

(**C 1**) This harbour town (pop. 90 000) on the north coast of the Cotentin peninsula is one of the busiest Channel ports. Cherbourg was conceived as a port and trading centre. It had substantial defences during the Hundred Years' War, but these were destroyed at the end of the 17th century. The great military architect Sébastien Vauban recognized the strategic importance of the town and drew up plans for a long breakwater and jetties. In 1853 the breakwater was finally complete and in 1858 Napoleon III opened a new naval base. The great naval tradition remains unbroken; Cherbourg is home to the third largest base in France for the country's fleet. In its heyday, Cherbourg welcomed all the grand Transatlantic cruise-liners in style. Nowadays, the maritime traffic mostly consists of ferries and yachts. The post-war rebuilding was not as imaginative as it could have been. Cherbourg is essentially a modern town, but though it is not a particularly attractive place it does have some interesting corners.

SIGHTS

Abbaye du Voeu
The extensive damage inflicted on this abbey (founded in 1145) during World War II has since been repaired. The refectory and the gardens are open to visitors.
Rue de l'Abbaye

Bassin du Commerce
The oldest part of the harbour complex (1831) is the restored old town. The streets of the *Quartier des Halles* are a nice place to go for a leisurely stroll, stopping off for a drink or even a meal. A little further on is the international *Chantereyne* marina. You can continue your walk along the town beach, though swimming off it is definitely not recommended.

Fort du Roule
◁▷ For a panoramic view of the town and docks, climb up to this 19th-century fortress on top of the 112-m high *Montagne de Roule*.

Parc Emmanuel Liais
These gardens contain some interesting tropical plant specimens.
Daily (except Mon) 10.00-12.00 and 14.00-17.00; 22 Rue de la Bucaille; Entrance: 10 FF

Sainte-Trinité
The basilica of Sainte-Trinité (14th/15th century), built in the Flamboyant Gothic style, is most unusual. The stately tower was a late, 19th-century addition.

MUSEUMS

Musée de la Liberation
A collection of interesting maps, documents and displays on the last year of war from D-Day to German surrender.
April-Sept daily 10.00-18.00, Oct-Mar daily (except Mon) 09.30-12.00 and 14.00-17.30; Entrance: 20 FF

Musée Thomas-Henry
This gallery has a fine collection of European paintings (15th-19th century) by artists including Fra Angelico, Filippo Lippi and Jean-François Millet.
Daily (except Mon) 09.00-12.00 and 14.00-18.00; Centre Culturel; Entrance: 15 FF

RESTAURANT

Chez Pain
Tasty fresh fish dishes in a comfortable restaurant. Good value.
59 Rue au Blé; Tel: 02 33 53 67 64; Category 3

HOTELS

Chantereyne
Hotel with sea views, right by the harbour.
50 rooms; Port de Plaisance; Tel: 02 33 93 02 20, Fax: 02 33 93 45 29; Category 2

Liberté
Good hotel with restaurant.
73 rooms; Rue G Sorel; Tel: 02 33 43 72 00, Fax: 02 33 20 01 32; Category 2

Mercure
Modern inn; views of the marina.
84 rooms; Gare Maritime; Tel: 02 33 44 01 11, Fax: 02 33 44 51 00; Category 2

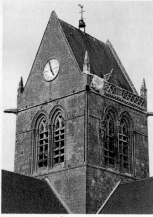

Sainte-Mère-Église

Chantereyne is France's second-largest marina with berths for 1500 yachts. It is also the venue for international boat shows.
Capitainerie du Port, Tel: 02 33 87 65 70, Fax: 02 33 53 21 12

In the *Casino*, right by the *Bassin du Commerce*, the dice continue to roll well into the night.

Maison du Tourisme
2 Quai Alexandre III; Tel: 02 33 93 52 02, Fax: 02 33 53 66 97

Barfleur (C 1)
★ A picturesque and lively fishing port and favourite haunt among the yachting fraternity. Mussels are still cultivated in the area, though their stocks are diminishing. On a great rock at the end of the harbour stands the rather forbidding church of *Saint-Nicolas* (17th century).

⚓ The coast road leads to the *Pointe de Barfleur*, the north-eastern tip of the Cotentin peninsula. It is crowned by the *Gatteville lighthouse* (1834) which at 75 m is the tallest in France (2 km from Barfleur).

Beaumont-Hague (B-C 1)
In the heart of the rugged *Cap Hague* landscape, on a 300-hectare plateau is the gigantic nuclear power station and reprocessing plant of Beaumont. Further south in Flamanville is a second nuclear power station. Both complexes can be visited by appointment (*Comega, Établissement de la Hague; Apr-Sept daily 10.00-19.00; Tel: 02 33 02 61 04*).

Bricquebec (C 2)
A romantic little town with a remarkably well-preserved 13th-century castle. The 22 m-high eleven-sided *donjon* (14th century) and the defensive walls are impressive. The 13th-century vaulted chapel has been lovingly restored, and the clock tower houses a small museum (*in summer daily, except Tues, 10.00-12.00 and 14.00-18.30, at other times by appointment; Tel: 02 33 52 21 13; Entrance: 7 FF*) and within the castle is a good hotel (*Vieux Château; 20 rooms; 4 Cours du Château; Tel: 02 33 52 24 49, Fax: 02 33 52 62 71; Category 2*). The *Abbaye Notre-Dame-de-Grâce* is a monastery occupied by Trappist monks (*access permitted once a day only at 15.30*).

Martinvast (C 1)
★ *Château Martinvast*, designated a *monument historique*, was origi-

nally a Norman fortress, updated in the Renaissance and again in the 19th century. The grounds, laid out in the English style with lakes and cascades, are well worth a visit. Special events in the summer include a *son et lumière* show.
In summer 14.00-19.00, at other times weekends only 14.00-18.00; Entrance: 30 FF

Saint-Germain-des-Vaux (B 1)

A small, windswept village just inland from the craggy *Cap de la Hague*, the most north-westerly tip of the Cotentin peninsula crowned by a towering lighthouse. The *Jardin Jacques Prévert* in the village itself has some rare tree species. ◁▷ The *Nez de Jobourg* just south of here is a great place to view the treacherous rocks and crashing waves.

Sainte-Mère-Église (C 2)

★ This was the first place the American troops liberated in 1944. The effigy of an American paratrooper that hangs from the belfry of the village church (11th-15th century) is an unusual D-Day memorial — and the subject of many a holiday snap. The *Musée des Troupes Aéroportées* documents the Normandy landings (*daily 10.00-12.00 and 14.00-18.00; Place du 6 Juin; Entrance: 20 FF*).

Saint-Vaast-la-Hougue (C 2)

★ In the Battle of Hougue in 1694 the French suffered a crushing defeat at the hands of the English. To strengthen their defences, they rebuilt the fortifications and harbour. The 17th-century fort with its imposing central tower and 3 m-thick walls demonstrates the skill of the military architects of the time. Such solid defences

enabled the seafaring town to develop undisturbed for centuries. The mild climate, sandy beach and oyster beds have ensured the continued popularity of this historic little fishing port (pop. 2500).

Two recommended hotel/restaurants here are the *Hôtel de France et des Fuchsias (32 rooms; 18 Rue du Maréchal-Foch; Tel: 02 33 54 42 26, Fax: 02 33 43 46 79; Category 2-3)* and *La Granitière (10 rooms; 64 Rue du Maréchal-Foch; Tel: 02 33 54 58 99, Fax: 02 33 20 34 91; Category 1-2).*

Just off shore is the *Île de Tatihou.* Crowned with a compact 18th-century fortress, the island is now a bird sanctuary. A regular ferry service departs from the harbour, although the number of visitors is strictly controlled. For further information contact *Accueil Tatihou, Quai Vauban, 50550 Saint-Vaast-la-Hougue; Tel: 02 33 23 19 92, Fax: 02 33 54 33 47.*

Tourlaville (C 1)

As you stroll through the grounds of this Italian Renaissance-style château (16th century) you'll come across some charming 19th-century summer-houses. Palms and colourful flowers evoke a tropical atmosphere.
Park: daily 10.00-12.00 and 14.00-17.00, in summer until 18.00; Entrance: free

Urville-Nacqueville (C 1)

This 16th-century manor house, tucked away in a valley near the hamlet of La Rivière, is impressive both for its beautiful façades and flower-filled park. It also has a lovely, photogenic 16th-century gatehouse.
Easter-30 Sept daily (except Tues and Thurs); Entrance: 25 FF

Utah Beach (C 2)

The westernmost landing beach in *Operation Overlord*, Utah beach, together with Omaha Beach (see page 67), was assigned to the American troops. A US memorial stands on the seafront.

Valognes (C 2)

The historic town of Valognes, once known as the 'Versailles of Normandy' (pop. 7000), was all but destroyed in 1944. Some scattered Gallo-Roman ruins, a handful of manor houses and churches dating from the 11th to the 18th century are the only proof left of its rich history. The main sights of the town are all in close proximity: the *Hôtel de Beaumont* (18th-century), the *Hôtel de Grandval-Caligny* (17th-18th century) and the *Maison du Grand Quartier* (15th century). The latter houses the *Musée Regional du Cidre* which recounts the 500-year history of the

traditional Normandy drink.
April-Sept daily (except Weds) 10.00-12.00 and 14.00-18.00; Entrance: 20 FF

MONT-SAINT-MICHEL

(B 4) ★ The ancient island monastery is the symbol of Normandy and one of the most famous buildings in France. Built on a granite mound in the *Baie du Mont-Saint-Michel,* this extraordinary 150 m edifice is visible from afar. Thousands of pilgrims in the Middle Ages came to marvel at it, and it continues to enthral millions of tourists today. But the sea has long since withdrawn from the mound, which is now reached along a 1.5 km causeway. The bay is threatening to silt up; only at the equinox high tide does the rocky island jut out of the waves. According to legend, Bishop Aubert of Avranches was

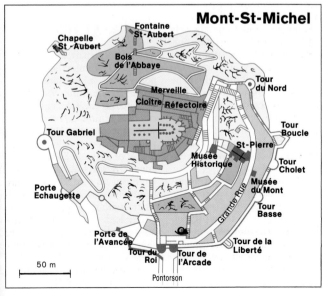

Mont-St-Michel

commanded by the Archangel Michael in 708 to construct a chapel on the island of *Mont Tombe*. The first Benedictine abbey was founded in 966, and in an eventful history spanning centuries one building on top of another was erected. In 1897 the Mont-Saint-Michel received its crowning glory with the gilded statue of the Archangel Michael which was placed on the pinnacle of the abbey church.

The tour of the complex starts at the *Porte de l'Avancée*. The hotels, restaurants, crêperies and souvenir shops concentrated along here are always full of people. The crowds thin out as you make the climb to the monastic buildings: the small chapel of *Saint-Aubert* (13th/14th century) perched on a rocky outcrop; the 11th-century abbey church and its crypts; and, most importantly, the Gothic fortress abbey known as *La Merveille* (The Marvel) with its majestic Knights' Hall, Guests' Hall and Refectory. The unique cloisters are arguably the best part of the whole complex. Designed for peace and meditation, they are 'close to heaven' and full of light. The beautiful gallery arcades with their pointed arches decorated in the Norman style rest on double rows of slender columns. ☟ The west terrace is the best vantage point offering spectacular views over the bay, coast and sea.

Other sights on the island include the *maritime museum*, the *wax museum*, and the *abbey gardens*. If you're visiting in high season you may find you have to queue for a while as access is limited to avoid over-crowding.
May-Sept daily 09.00-17.30, Oct-April 09.30-16.30; Entrance: 37 FF

RESTAURANT

La Mère Poulard
The famous omelettes of this respected establishment on the Mount are as much a part of the experience as the abbey itself.
Grande Rue; Tel: 02 33 60 14 01; Category 1

HOTEL

Saint-Pierre
Hotel in a half-timbered building at the foot of the monastery complex, with a unique atmosphere and the added bonus of a good restaurant.
21 rooms; Grande Rue; Tel: 02 33 60 14 03, Fax: 02 33 48 59 83; Category 1

INFORMATION

Office de Tourisme
Lower Gateway; Tel: 02 33 60 14 30, Fax: 02 33 60 06 75

ST-LÔ

(**C 3**) The département capital (pop. 25 000) enjoys an elevated position on a prominent rock above the beautiful Vire valley. Founded in the 6th century, the city was almost completely destroyed in the war. Hundreds of years of history was lost in just a matter of days and St-Lô became known as 'the Capital of Ruins'. Unfortunately the reconstruction has not been as successful as elsewhere, with the exception of the skilful and sensitive restoration of the defensive walls and the church. Now an important agricultural centre, St-Lô is best-known for its national stud farm, the biggest in France.

SIGHTS

Haras National

★ East of the town is the Haras National, an extensive stud farm set up in 1806 by Napoleon and a French national treasure. Well over 100 stallions of various breeds are housed in beautifully-tended stables. Visitors are welcome.

In summer daily 14.00-17.00, at other times weekends 14.00-17.00; Avenue du Maréchal Juin; Entrance: 20 FF

Notre-Dame

At the heart of the town stands the church of Notre-Dame (13th-17th century). Built in the Flamboyant style, it suffered terrible damage during World War II, but it has been brilliantly restored. The external pulpit on the choir aisle and the sheer green wall with its modern bronze doors are particularly striking.

Town walls

◁▷ A walk around the old defensive walls, dominated by an imposing tower, leads to wonderful views over the Vire valley and the the 'bocage' countryside.

MUSEUM

Musée Municipal des Beaux-Arts

The star attraction of this museum housed in the town hall is the engaging series of tapestries (16th/17th century) depicting scenes of a carefree pastoral life. It also has a fine collection of 18th- and 19th-century paintings including works by Boudin, Corot and Millet.

Daily (except Tues) 10.00-12.00 and 14.00-18.00; Place du Champ de Mars; Entrance: 10 FF

RESTAURANT

Le Tocqueville

Small restaurant with good food and a welcoming atmosphere.

Place de la Gare; Tel: 02 33 05 08 63; Category 3

HOTELS

Relais Mercure

Friendly hotel, centrally located opposite the town walls.

34 rooms; 1 Avenue Briovère; Tel: 02 33 05 10 84, Fax: 02 33 56 46 92; Category 2

Parc Naturel Régional des Marais du Cotentin et du Bessin

The marshes and moorland of the Cotentin and Bessin areas form an extensive nature reserve, which supports a rich variety of flora and fauna. During the winter months these flat expanses of land are flooded by the sea. It is only from the spring onwards, when the waters recede, that the meadows dotted with rushes and reeds can be used as pasture for horses, cattle and sheep. One of the best ways to discover the marshland is on one of the organized boat trips which follow the course of the Douvre and Taute rivers down to the Baie des Veys. A tour of the area in a horse-drawn caravan is an interesting alternative. *Information is available from the Parc Naturel Régional des Marais du Cotentin et du Bessin, Manoir de Cantepie, 50500 Les Veys; Tel: 02 33 71 61 90, Fax: 02 33 71 61 91*

Les Voyageurs

Simple, good value hotel.

5/7 Avenue Briovère; Tel: 02 33 05 08 63, Fax: 02 33 05 14 34; Category 3

INFORMATION

Office de Tourisme

Place du Générale de Gaulle; Tel/Fax: 02 33 05 02 09

SURROUNDING AREA

Barneville-Carteret (B 2)

Sheltered by a rocky headland from the forces of the Alderney race (a notoriously strong current) and gently warmed by the Gulf Stream, this popular twin resort (pop. 2500) on the west Cotentin coast enjoys a mild, temperate climate. Ferries ply daily in summer between the neighbouring Channel Islands (Jersey is just 25 km away) and the busy little fishing port of Cartaret. Barneville, its more peaceful counterpart on the other side of the bay, has a beautiful stretch of clean, white sandy beach backed by high dunes. It also has an 11th-century Romanesque church with some finely decorated capitals.

☙ The *Rue du Cap* leads out to the lighthouse on the Cap de Carteret, an excellent starting-point for bracing walks along the clifftops and beaches.

The restaurant of *Le Gohan*, housed in an old barn, has an ancient feel to it. The menu is based on fish and grills (*Rue au Lait; Tel: 02 33 04 95 33; Category 2*).

A recommended hotel is *La Marine* (*31 rooms; 11 Rue de Paris; Tel: 02 33 53 83 31, Fax: 02 33 53 39 60; Category 2*).

Carentan (C 2)

This old cathedral town (pop. 7000), the self-styled 'Gateway to the Cotentin', lies at the end of a long inlet. Surrounded by vast expanses of moorland and meadows, it is a major cattle and dairy farming centre for the region. ❖ A lively cattle market is held here every Monday. In the middle of this pleasant town stands the Gothic cathedral of Notre-Dame (11th-16th century); its fine octagonal spire can be seen for miles around. Also of interest is the 17th-century town hall housed in a former Augustinian monastery, and a row of 15th-century stone houses with impressive Gothic arcades.

A recommended hotel is the *Aire de la Baie (40 rooms; RN 13, Les Veys; Tel: 02 33 42 00 99, Fax: 02 33 71 06 94; Category 2).*

Cerisy-la-Forêt (D 3)

The main attraction of this forest hamlet is the Benedictine abbey of *Saint-Vigor* founded in the 6th century. Many of the monastery buildings have been preserved; the 11th-century abbey church is one of the finest examples of Romanesque architecture in Normandy. There is also a lapidary museum with a small collection of statues and wall and floor tiles from the 14th/15th century.

Easter-15 Nov daily 09.00-18.30; Entrance: 15 FF

Coutances (C 3)

On a gently sloping hill above the Prépont and Bulsard rivers lies the town of Coutances (pop. 13 000) which for centuries was the capital of the Cotentin. It consolidated its position of power with the magnificent *Cathedrale de*

Notre-Dame (13th/15th century). Built on the highest point of the hill, it is one of the most prominent landmarks in the area. With its tall twin towers and turreted lantern tower, it is an impressive example of the Norman Gothic tradition. The town hall is also of interest with its beautiful façade and formal terraced gardens (*Jardin des Plantes*).

A recommended hotel is the *Cositel* (*55 rooms; Route de Coutainville; Tel: 02 33 07 51 64, Fax: 02 33 07 06 23; Category 2-3*).

It's worth making a short detour to visit the moated *Château de Gratot* (14th-16th century), only 4 km away.

Hambye (C 3)

Tucked away in the heart of the Sienne valley, the Benedictine monks at the *Abbaye de Hambye* (12th century) enjoyed a peaceful existence for many centuries. Then, in the 17th century, the monastery began to fall into decline until it was eventually ruined and abandoned in the French Revolution. The few buildings left standing, however, give a good idea of the original size of what must once have been a magnificent monastery. Among the early Gothic remains are the shell of a church, a chapterhouse, a library and a kitchen, and some of the outbuildings in which animals were kept.

Daily (except Tues) 10.00-12.00 and 14.00-18.00; Entrance: 20 FF

Lessay

This small town (pop. 14 000) surrounded by heathland is centred around an important Benedictine monastery. The 11th-century ★ *Abbaye Sainte-Trinité* was carefully restored after World War II using traditional tools and methods. It features some fine Romanesque ribbed vaulting (*daily 08.00-19.00; Entrance: free*).

The surrounding moorland of *Mathon* is a thriving nature reserve; the habitat of many rare plants and insects and a good place for country walks.

Portbail (C 2)

This popular resort (pop. 17 000) marks the beginning of a long stretch of fine sandy beaches backed by dunes. Ferry services from the lively marina to the Channel Islands operate throughout the summer. The fortified church of *Notre-Dame* (11th century) by the harbour is worth a closer look.

Saint-Sauveur-le-Vicomte (C 2)

This fortified town in the heart of the Cotentin played an important role in the Hundred Years' War. The 11th-century fortress was badly damaged in 1944, but the defensive walls, prison tower and keep have been well preserved. To the south of the town is a Romanesque Benedictine abbey, home to the Order of the Sisters of Mercy since 1832 (*daily 10.00-12.00 and 14.30-17.00; Entrance: free*).

Troisgots-la-Chapelle-sur-Vire (C 3)

This has been a popular pilgrimage site ever since the 12th century. The chapel houses a memorable statue of *Notre-Dame-de-Vire* (15th century). Also worth adding to your itinerary is a visit to the imposing *Château Angotière* (16th-18th century) set in a magnificent park at the southern end of the village.

The Perche and Suisse Normande

The hills and forests make fine walking country

From the Suisse Normande in the north, an area of rivers, waterfalls and woods, through the valleys of the Perche to the Parc National Régional Normandie-Maine in the south, the countryside beyond the rugged cliffs and sandy beaches is a haven of rural peace. The Orne is a hilly region dotted with trees, hedges, meadows and small lakes, and plenty of beautiful châteaux, churches and abbeys. It is dominated by thickly wooded areas, from Reno-Valdieu in the east through Bellême, Saint-Evroult, Ecouves and Andaine, to Halouze in the west. The river Orne and all its tributaries meander through the middle of it all. There is a long tradition of horse-rearing in the area, and the studs here produce some of the finest European breeds, including Percherons. For those who enjoy walking, eating, fine architecture and a quiet life this is a perfect place to escape to.

The Orne countryside is ideal for horse-riding and hiking

ALENÇON

(E 5) The market town of Alençon (pop. 35 000) is the administrative centre of the département of Orne. It is situated on the southern border of Normandy in large expanses of forest (the Ecouves Forest, the Perseigne Forest and the Alpes Mancelles). As such it is an ideal base for exploring the surrounding country. Alençon is a centre of agriculture, with industry and commerce contributing to the local economy. The town's name is most famously associated with lace. The 'Point d'Alençon' technique has been practised since the 17th century, when it was developed to compete with the Venetian lace that was then worn by the ladies in court. This intricate craft is now a dying art. During World War II, Alençon was heavily bombarded, but the historic town centre remained relatively unscathed; most of what was damaged has since been restored. Wandering the pedestrianized streets is a pleasant way to while away some time.

Château des Ducs

The impressive 15th-century town castle, with its two massive towers, opens on to the *Place Foch*. Once the elegant court of dukes and nobles, it is now a jail. It was first used as a prison by the Gestapo and many French patriots were tortured and killed within its walls.

Maison d'Ozé

This 15th-century manor house is one of the town's finest buildings. It now houses the *Office de Tourisme* and exhibitions on local history. *Daily 09.00-18.30; Place Lamagdelaine*

Notre-Dame

The church of Notre-Dame in the centre of town was built in the 15th century in the Flamboyant Gothic style. Its most outstanding features are the stained-glass windows (16th century) in the nave and the elaborate portal. The tower, crossing, transept and chancel were faithfully restored after a fire in the 18th century.

Mon-Sat 08.30-12.00 and 14.00-17.30, Sun 09.00-12.00 and 14.30-17.00; Place Lamagdelaine

Saint-Léonard

The narrow streets and alleys of the quaint old Saint-Léonard quarter at the heart of the town are lined with medieval half-timbered houses. Take a leisurely stroll through the streets and admire the beautiful façades, windows, and balconies with their wrought-iron balustrades, not forgetting the lovely church of *Saint-Léonard* (15th century).

MUSEUMS

Musée de la Dentelle au Point d'Alençon

★ The history and technique of Point d'Alençon lace-making are explained in some depth. Take a close look at the intricate pieces of lace on display; the amount of skill and patience required to produce such finely detailed work soon becomes apparent.
Daily (except Sun and bank holidays) 10.00-12.00 and 14.00-18.00; 31 Rue du Pont-Neuf; Entrance: 20 FF

MARCO POLO SELECTION: ORNE

1 Point d'Alençon
Delicate hand-made lace can be admired in Alençon's two lace museums (pages 84 and 85)

2 Château d'O
A graceful moated castle in Motrée (page 86)

3 Le Pin-au-Haras
Surrounded by forest, this is one of Europe's most important studs (page 87)

4 Saint-Céneri-le-Gérei
Overlooking the slopes of the Alpes Mancelles, this picturesque site has been classified as one of the '100 most beautiful villages in France' (page 87)

5 Sées cathedral
The towering cathedral on the banks of the Orne is a masterpiece of Norman High Gothic (page 87)

Musée des Beaux-Arts et de la Dentelle

★ Alongside its collection of hand-made lace, this museum also houses works by French painters from the 17th to the 20th century. *Daily (except Mon) 10.00-12.00 and 14.00-18.00; 12 Rue Charles-Avelin; Entrance: 16 FF*

L'Escargot Doré

Fine regional cuisine. *183 Avenue du Général Leclerc; Tel: 02 33 28 67 67; Category 2*

There are some good shops in the pedestrianized streets. Naturally, you'll see lace displayed in shop windows all over the place, but if you want to be sure of buying the genuine hand-made article, your safest bet is the museum shop.

Le Grand Cerf

A comfortable inn with a reasonably priced restaurant. *20 rooms; 21 Rue Saint-Blaise; Tel: 02 33 26 00 51, Fax: 02 33 26 63 07; Category 2*

♣ If you want to liven up your evening, the choice is between the *L'Arc en Ciel* disco (*11 Rue de la Halle aux Toiles*) or music at the *La Luciole* café (*171 Rue de Bretagne*).

Office de Tourisme

Place Lamagdelaine; Tel: 02 33 26 11 36, Fax: 02 33 32 10 53

Argentan   (E 4)

Another town on the Orne (pop. 18 000) which gained its reputation through lace-making. The *Point d'Argentan* tradition is still alive here and you can watch the lace-makers at work (*daily, except Sun, 10.30-12.00 and 14.30-16.30; Entrance: 10 FF*).

Few of Argentan's historic buildings were left standing after World War II. Among the architectural treasures salvaged from the rubble were the churches of *Saint-Germain* (15th-17th century) and *Saint Martin* (15th-16th century) both built in the Flamboyant style. All that remains of the medieval castle is the ruined 12th-century *donjon*.

Bellême   (F 5)

On a hilltop overlooking the *Forêt de Bellême*, this historic town (pop. 1800) is the capital of the Perche district. It is worth exploring on foot. The principal sights include the remains of the town's defences, the 15th-century main gate flanked by towers, the church of *Saint-Sauveur* (15th-17th century) and some fine 17th/18th-century town houses. Among the old alleyways is the charming *Rue Ville-Close*.

Carrouges   (E 5)

Set in the middle of an extensive park, the vast moated Château de Carrouges (14th-17th century) is one of France's most outstanding castles. Its unique charm stems from the juxtaposition of styles and building materials applied over three centuries. Highlights are the 14th-century *donjon* and the slender 16th-century gatehouse with its gabled roof and round towers.

Daily 10.00-11.30 and 14.00-17.30; Entrance: 32 FF

Château d'O (E 5)

★ An excursion to the enchanting Château d'O (15th-17th century) is a must. Designed as an aristocratic residence, its style is predominantly Flamboyant. The tall slate turrets and brick and stone walls of this fairy-tale castle are reflected in the waters of the surrounding wide moat (*daily, except Tues, 14.30-17.00, in summer until 18.00; Entrance: 30 FF*).

Just 4 km away, on the edge of the *Ecouves* forest, in the village of *Saint-Christophe-le-Jajolet* is the *Château de Sassy* (18th century). Set in terraced gardens, with a beautiful lake, the castle is worth visiting to see the grounds alone (*April-Oct daily 15.00-18.00; park all year; Entrance: 25 FF*).

The turreted Château d'O at Mortrée near Sées

Domfront (D 4)

This small medieval town (pop. 4500) steeped in history towers 135 m above the *Varenne valley*. The former stronghold (11th century) was destroyed by Henri IV. The ruins and remaining towers of the town's old defensive walls are a picturesque sight in their leafy parkland setting. Like so many medieval Norman towns, Domfront is characterized by narrow streets and half-timbered houses and it has a fine Romanesque church, the *Notre-Dame-sur-l'Eau* which stands by the river (*daily 09.00-18.00*).

Le Pin-au-Haras (E 4)

★ This 18th-century Château owned by the National stud, is striking in its simple elegance. The castle is not open to visitors, but the horseshoe-shaped inner courtyard and the stables are. *April-Oct daily 09.30-18.00, at other times daily 10.00-12.00 and 14.00-17.00; Entrance: 25 FF*

Mortagne-au-Perche (F 5)

〽 Perched on a high hill, the quiet capital of the Perche region (pop. 5000) looks down over the rolling green countryside. The finest views can be seen from the *Jardin Public*. The town's central landmark is the *Église Notre-Dame* (15th-century), a combination of Flamboyant and early Renaissance styles. The interior wood-panelling (18th century) is particularly noteworthy. The pretty cloister of the *Hôpital Hospice*, a former Franciscan foundation, is also worth a look. Mortagne is most famous for its *boudin noir*, a delicious type of black pudding which can be bought at the specialist market here.

Saint-Céneri-le-Gérei (E 5)

★ This little hilltop village in a picturesque setting above a bend in the Sarthe river has been classified as one of the '100 most beautiful villages in France'. 〽 It merits this title both for the breathtaking views it presents over the slopes of the *Alpes Mancelles*, and for the charm of its streets and alleyways, its ancient bridge, and above all for its unusual *Romanesque church*, one of Normandy's gems. It was designed as a passage church, and has a lantern tower between the transepts. The banks of the Sarthe offer excellent fishing.

Sées (E 5)

★ The history of this ancient cathedral town (pop. 5000) on the banks of the Orne, goes right back to the 4th century. It is centred around the imposing cathedral of *Notre-Dame* (13th century) whose two tall spires dominate the area. The cathedral itself has a colourful history, and is considered a masterpiece of Norman High Gothic (*daily 09.30-17.00*).

A recommended hotel here is *Le Dauphin* (*7 rooms; 32 Place des Halles; Tel: 02 33 27 8 07, Fax: 02 33 28 80 33; Category 2*).

Soligny-la-Trappe (F 5)

In the hilly Perche country by the little village of *Soligny* is the 12th-century abbey where the rules of the strict Trappist order (named after the *Trappe* forest) were established by the Cistercian abbot, De Rancé (1626-1700). The monks support themselves by selling all kinds of their own produce; the abbey shop is a good reason to visit the 19th-century complex, otherwise closed to visitors.

Practical information

*Important addresses and useful information
for your visit to Normandy*

BANKS

In cities and larger towns normal opening hours are *Mon-Fri, 09.00-16.30/17.00*. In smaller places banks are *closed for lunch from 12.30-13.30/14.00* and *on Mon*, but *open on Sat 09.00-12.00* instead. The range of services provided, exchange rates and commission charged are similarly variable.

Credit cards (especially Visa and Mastercard/Eurocard) are increasingly widely accepted, and can also be used to withdraw cash from banks; best exchange rates are obtained from cash machines (don't forget your PIN number). Eurocheques can currently be cashed up to the value of 1400 FF. Presentation of your passport is required for all bank transactions.

CAMPING

Normandy has a wide choice of campsites, ranging from the basically equipped to the luxury class, complete with swimming pool and restaurant. There is also a number of designated *Aires naturelles de camping* (small sites in more remote rural locations) or,

if you can do without facilities, *Camping à la ferme* (on designated areas of farmland) is a cheaper option. Camping in unauthorized areas is not permitted. Detailed information about campsites in the area is available from: *Comité Régional du Tourisme de Normandie, 14 Rue Charles Corbeau, 27000 Evreux; Tel: 02 32 33 79 00*

CHEMISTS

A *pharmacie* is indicated by a green cross which flashes when the chemist is open. Normal opening hours are *09.00-12.30 and 14.00-18.30*. A list of chemists on duty for late-night and weekend opening should be posted on the door. French pharmacists are well qualified and can usually be consulted for minor ailments. A wide range of medicines is available over the counter without prescription.

CONSULATES/EMBASSIES

French Consulate General
in England: *1, Cromwell Place, London SW7, Tel: 0171 581 5292*
in Scotland: *7, Randolph Crescent, Edinburgh, Tel: 0131 225 7954*

in Ireland: *36, Ailesbury Road, Dublin 4, Tel: 01 694777*
in the USA: *4101/Reservoir Rd NW, Washington DC 20007. Tel: 202 944 6000*

Consulates/Embassies in France
British Consulate: *16 Rue d'Anjou, 75008 Paris, Tel: 01 45 00 20 87*
Irish Embassy: *4 Rue Rude, 75016 Paris, Tel: 01 45 00 20 87*
American Consulate: *2 Rue St Florentin, 75001 Paris, Tel: 01 42 96 12 02*

CUSTOMS

Although customs restrictions have now been lifted for goods imported between EU countries (provided they are for personal use), there are certain recommended restrictions: 800 cigarettes, 90 litres wine, 10 litres spirits. For non-EU countries the personal allowances are: 1 litre spirits or 2 litres fortified wine or 3 l table wine; 200 cigarettes or 100 cigarillos or 50 cigars.

VAT (TVA) on the purchase of luxury goods (eg jewellery) will be partially refunded by the French authorities, though it is a complicated and time-consuming process. Information can be obtained from relevant shops or the customs office.

CYCLING

Normandy is perfect cycling country. Bicycles can be hired at railway stations (look for the sign *train + velo*). The best map for route planning is the *Michelin sheet No. 231 Normandie*. Suggested routes are available from the local *Offices de Tourisme* and from the *Fédération Française de Cyclotourisme,* 8 *Rue Jean-Marie-Jego, 75013 Paris; Tel: 01 44 16 88 88.*

DOCTORS

In an emergency, the police can tell you where to find the nearest duty doctor (*Tel: 17*). A visit to the doctor costs between 120 FF and 150 FF and has to be paid for immediately. Fees will be reimbursed by your local health authority provided you have an E111 form (available from the post office), but the application involves a lot of red tape. You are well advised to take out comprehensive medical insurance.

DRIVING

The French do drive very fast, even in built-up areas. Although police checks are rare, exceeding the speed limits will incur quite heavy fines. Speed limits are: motorways 130 km/h, 110 km/h in rain; dual carriageways 110 km/h, 100 km/h in rain; national and département roads (N, D) 90 km/h, 80 km/h in rain; built-up areas 50 km/h. Recently qualified drivers who have less than a year's experience are limited to a speed of 90 km/h. Seat-belts must be worn by both driver and passengers. Motorbikes must be driven with dipped headlights at all times and this applies to all traffic in rain and fog.

Tolls are payable on motorways; at the current rate, allow for around 35 FF per 100 km. The French road network is excellent and routes are clearly signposted, so that orientation is relatively easy. However, traffic on the *Routes Nationales* (primary routes) can get quite heavy, especially in the French holiday season (July and August).

In the case of an accident, the police must be called if anyone is injured (*Tel: 17*). Breakdown assistance (*dépanneur-remorquer*) can be summoned via the police or emergency call-boxes on motorways.

Unleaded petrol (*sans plomb*), is available at most filling stations and is less expensive than 4-star (*super*). Minor car problems can be dealt with at most filling station workshops.

ELECTRICITY

The voltage in France is 220 V and the plugs are two-pin so remember to take an adaptor for your small appliances.

EMERGENCY NUMBERS

Police: *Police Secours, Tel: 17*
Fire service: *Tel: 15*
Medical emergencies: *Tel: 15*

FISHING

With so many inland lakes and rivers, angling is a popular sport in Normandy. Information on the rules and regulations can be obtained from the *Fédération Départementale des Associations de Pêche et de Pisciculture*. Rod licences and licences to fish private waters are available from the *commune* at the local *mairie* (town hall).

INFORMATION

**Maison de la France –
French Government Tourist Office**
UK: *178, Piccadilly, London W1V 0AL; Tel. 0171 491 7622*

Ireland: *35, Lower Abbey Street, Dublin 1; Tel. 01 703 4046, Fax 01 874 7324*

USA: *610 Fifth Avenue, Suite 222, New York, NY 10020-2452; Tel. 212 757 1125*

The beaches by the northern cliffs are the most popular family resorts

The Suisse Normande

The 'Switzerland of Normandy' is a green and hilly – though not exactly mountainous! – area of Calvados, which starts about 20 km south of Caen. The well-signposted *Route de la Suisse Normande* wends its way past rolling hills, wooded valleys and steep rocky escarpments, rivers, lakes and streams. The river Orne runs right through the middle of this picturesque region, carving its way through the rocks, sometimes slow and smooth, sometimes torrential. The circular route goes from Thury-Harcourt via Condé-sur-Noireau, Pont d'Ouilly and Clécy, back to Thury-Harcourt, linking castles, churches, chapels and villages. If you are feeling energetic, there are plenty of opportunities here for walking and mountain biking. Other activities on offer in the region include horse-riding, hang-gliding, climbing and canoeing. For further information contact the *Office de Tourisme, 14220 Thury-Harcourt, Place Saint-Sauveur; Tel: 02 31 79 70 45.*

You'll find a *Syndicat d'Initiative* in every town and most villages. The tourist office covering the whole of Normandy is:
Comité Régional du Tourisme Normandie; 14 Rue Charles Corbeau, 27000 Evreux; Tel: 02 32 33 79 00, Fax: 02 32 31 19 04

NATURISM

The French are great fans of *naturisme*. On the coast of Normandy numerous remote beaches and bays have been set aside for nudists. These *Domaines Naturistes* can be found at star-rated campsites, a number of hotels, and some sports and leisure centres. The *Guide Naturiste Français* contains addresses and descriptions of the sites and is available from *Socnat, 16 Rue Drouot, 75009 Paris.*

NEWSPAPERS

In the larger towns, the *Maisons de Presse*, newsagents and tobacconists, stock a wide range of French and foreign newspapers

and magazines, including a limited selection of British ones which are usually available the day after publication.

OPENING HOURS

Fresh baguettes can be bought from the bakery from *07.00*, sometimes even as early as *06.30*. Grocers open around *08.00*, department stores and boutiques at *09.00* or *10.00* at the latest. Apart from the hypermarkets and shopping centres, most shops close for lunch from *12.00-14.00* and then stay open until *19.00/19.30*. Bakers and larger stores are also open on Sunday mornings, but the majority of shops are closed all day on Monday.

POST & TELEPHONES

Post offices *(Poste or PTT)* are open *Mon-Fri 09.00-12.00* and *14.00-17.00, Sat 09.00-12.00.* You can also buy postage stamps *(timbres)* from the many tobacconist shops *(tabac)*.

Long-distance and international calls can be made from any phone box or from the booths in post offices. Most public phones will take phone cards (*télécarte*), which come in units of 50 (40 FF) or 120 (96 FF). You can buy them from tobacconists, post offices, filling stations and hotels. Local calls from a kiosk cost 1 FF per minute; long-distance calls to most western European countries cost around 5 FF per minute. Cheap rate is *Mon-Fri 21.30-08.00, Sat from 14.00* and *all day Sun*. To phone abroad from France, dial 00 followed by the country code (UK: 44, Ireland: 353, USA 1) the area code omitting the initial 0, and the subscriber number. To phone France from abroad dial 00 33, followed by the regional code (2 for Normandy) and the eight-digit subscriber number.

PUBLIC TRANSPORT

Public transport in France is generally very reliable and efficient. The national railway network

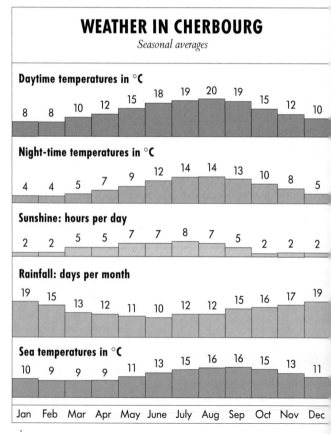

WEATHER IN CHERBOURG
Seasonal averages

Daytime temperatures in °C

Jan	Feb	Mar	Apr	May	June	July	Aug	Sep	Oct	Nov	Dec
8	8	10	12	15	18	19	20	19	15	12	10

Night-time temperatures in °C

Jan	Feb	Mar	Apr	May	June	July	Aug	Sep	Oct	Nov	Dec
4	4	5	7	9	12	14	14	13	10	8	5

Sunshine: hours per day

Jan	Feb	Mar	Apr	May	June	July	Aug	Sep	Oct	Nov	Dec
2	2	5	5	7	7	8	7	5	2	2	2

Rainfall: days per month

Jan	Feb	Mar	Apr	May	June	July	Aug	Sep	Oct	Nov	Dec
19	15	13	12	11	10	12	12	15	16	17	19

Sea temperatures in °C

Jan	Feb	Mar	Apr	May	June	July	Aug	Sep	Oct	Nov	Dec
10	9	9	9	11	13	15	16	16	15	13	11

A view of the River Orne near Pont d'Ouilly

(SNCF) is excellent: trains are fast, services frequent and fares very reasonable. Before buying your ticket, it's worth enquiring about special discounts and rail passes. Before getting on the train, remember to have your ticket punched by one of the machines on the station concourse.

The railway network is backed up in the rural areas by a comprehensive bus network. This means that you can get to most places quickly and easily by train and/or bus. In the larger towns, the bus station (*gare routière*) is usually near the train station. Route maps and timetables are available from the local tourist office.

TIPPING

In hotels, a 10 FF tip is the norm for, say, calling a taxi or carrying luggage. In the case of extended stays the chambermaid should also be tipped (from 10-20 FF per week). In restaurants, taxis and at the hairdresser, 10% is customary.

TRAVEL DOCUMENTS

EU and North American citizens can stay in France for up to 90 days with a valid passport. EU citizens wishing to stay in the country for more than three months must apply for a *Carte de Séjour.*

YOUTH HOSTELS

There is a wide choice of good youth hostels in the region. You have to be a member of the international YHA, but there is no age limit. For further information contact the *YHA, Trevelyan House, 8 St Stephen's Hill, St Alban's, Herts AL1; Tel: 01727 845047* or the *Fédération Unie des Auberges de Jeunesse, 27 Rue Pajol, 75018 Paris; Tel: 01 44 89 87 27.*

Do's and don'ts

How to avoid some of the dangers and pitfalls that face the unwary traveller

No vacancies

In July and August, the whole country goes *en vacances*, so accommodation, especially in the coastal resorts, gets booked up well in advance. If you are planning on travelling at this time of year, hotel rooms, holiday homes, apartments and campsites will need to be booked well in advance. Finding a place to stay at any other time, however, will be much easier – and cheaper. Remember that many places close up for the winter, especially in the seaside resorts.

Dangerous tides

At ebb tide (roughly every six hours) the sea recedes a long way, but then it flows back dangerously fast. It's always a good idea to check the tides before embarking on a beach walk. Knowledgeable locals or the tourist office can give advice, and tide timetables are also available.

Swimming in the sea

Before diving headlong into the waves you should take the time to get acquainted with the sea, especially on quiet beaches without a lifeguard on duty. On beaches surrounded by rocks and cliffs the incoming waves are subject to strong currents and treacherous shallows which can endanger even the most experienced swimmer. The same applies to windsurfing and sailing, where the powerful waves and strong winds also take their toll on equipment. If in doubt, check with the local tourist office or coastguard which stretches of coast are safe for bathing or water sports.

Petty crime

Tourists are prime targets for pickpockets and petty thieves. While the crime rate is relatively low in Normandy, it pays to be cautious. Cars and their contents are most at risk, especially if they are parked in out-of-the-way places where there are few potential witnesses. Always make sure your car is securely locked and any valuables hidden away from view, preferably in a locked boot.

Dress codes

As a mark of respect, avoid wearing skimpy clothing when visiting an abbey, cathedral or church.

INDEX

This index lists all the places mentioned in this guide. Page numbers in bold indicate the main entry in the case of multiple references, italics indicate photos

What do you get for your money?

 The unit of currency is the French franc (FF), which is divided into 100 centimes. Bank notes come in denominations of 20, 50, 100, 200 and 500 FF and there are coins of 1, 2, 5, 10 and 20 FF, and 5, 10, 20 and 50 centimes.

Accommodation prices are highest in July and August; prices in June and September are often reduced by as much as 30%.

Motorway (*autoroute*) tolls work out at around 35 FF per 100 km. Petrol costs around 6.20 FF per litre (unleaded); the cheapest places to fill up are supermarket filling stations.

For quality and value, the weekly markets are the best places for food shopping. The hypermarkets on the outskirts of the bigger towns and cities also stock an excellent range of reasonably priced provisions.

In a restaurant, you get a better deal all round if you order food from a fixed menu rather than *à la carte*. A good value three-course meal costs from around 80 FF, and an accompanying bottle of quality wine will add about 90 FF to the bill.

A *café noir* to end the meal will cost about 10 FF. A fresh *baguette* from the baker (*boulangerie*) can cost as little as 3.50 FF.

£	FF	FF	£
1	9.80	5	0.51
2	19.60	10	1.02
3	29.40	15	1.53
4	39.20	20	2.04
5	49.00	25	2.55
6	58.80	30	3.06
7	68.60	35	3.57
8	78.40	40	4.08
9	88.20	50	5.10
10	98.00	75	7.65
15	147.00	100	10.20
20	196.00	150	15.30
25	245.00	200	20.40
30	294.00	250	25.50
40	392.00	300	30.60
50	490.00	500	51.00
75	735.00	750	76.50
100	980.00	1000	102.00
250	2450.00	5000	510.20
500	4900.00	7500	765.30
1000	9800.00	10000	1020.40

The conversion table above is based on the Thomas Cook tourist rate, November 97